24 Colorful Jewelry Projects

Kathy Fox

The Venetian Glass Bead

24 Colorful Jewelry Projects

Kathy Fox

Kalmbach Books
21027 Crossroads Circle
Waukesha, Wisconsin 53186
www.Kalmbach.com/Books

Published in 2012
16 15 14 13 12   1 2 3 4 5

Manufactured in the United States of America

ISBN: 978-0-87116-415-5

Editor: *Karin Van Voorhees*
Art Director: *Lisa Bergman*
Proofreader: *Elisa Neckar*
Graphic Designer: *Rebecca Markstein*
Photographers: *William Zuback, James Forbes*

Publisher's Cataloging-in-Publication Data

Fox, Kathy.
The Venetian glass bead : 24 colorful jewelry projects / Kathy Fox.

p. : col. ill. ; cm.

Includes bibliographical references.
ISBN: 978-0-87116-415-5

1. Beadwork–Handbooks, manuals, etc. 2. Beadwork–Patterns. 3. Glass beads–Italy–Murano. 4. Jewelry making. I. Title.

TT860 .F68 2012
745.594/2

Contents

Introduction 6

History of Venezia 8

The Glassmaking Industry 10

History of Trade Beads 12

Making Venetian Glass Beads 14

Chapter 1

Traditional Venetian Glass Beads 16
Bella Vita Necklace & Earrings 18
Madonna dell'Orto Rosary 20
Giovanni Leather Necklace 22
Art Nouveau Coil Bracelet 24
Conterie 27

Chapter 2

Modern Venetian Glass Beads 28
Cipriani Bracelet & Earrings 30
Venetian Foil Beads 32
Ca' d'Oro Necklace & Earrings 33
Midnight Skies Necklace & Earrings 36
Danieli Necklace & Earrings 38
Lucia Wrap Bracelet 40
Vivaldi Ring 42
Rezzonico Necklace & Earrings 44
Golden Mosaic Necklace & Earrings 46
Missoni, Miro, and Klimt 49
Acqua Alta Necklace & Earrings 50
How to Spot Imitations 52

Chapter 3

Designing with Venetian Glass Beads 54
Jewels of Venice Foil Lentil Knotted Necklace 56
Nero Bianco Crocheted Necklace 59
Farfalla Viking Knit Bracelet 62
Designing with Venetian Beads on a Budget 65
Enchanted Life Necklace 66
Vicenza Splendor Necklace 68

Chapter 4

Travels to Venice 70
Piazza San Marco 72
Torre dell'Orologio 74
Steampunk Torre dell'Orologio Necklace 75
Campanile di San Marco 77
Casanova Necklace & Earrings 78
Palazzo Ducale 81
Basillica di San Marco 82
San Marco Necklace & Earrings 84
La Fenice Opera House 87
La Fenice Necklace & Earrings 88
Lagoon 90
Salvation Bracelet 94
Mediterranean Necklace & Earrings 96

Basics

Basic Beading Techniques 102

References, Photo Credits, Project Sources, and Measurement Conversion 108

About the Author 110

Acknowledgments 111

Introduction

It was one of those things that changed my life forever. During a vacation in the summer of 2002, my daughter's aunt invited her to go to a local bead store and make jewelry for her birthday. I was unfamiliar with the concept of making your own jewelry, so I went along. As we entered the store, I was awestruck. I had never seen so many beads in my life. There were beads everywhere—made from glass, silver, gold, pewter, crystal, stone, and more. At first it was overwhelming, but it turned out to be an amazing experience as we laughed and talked with each other for hours while we created our beautiful jewelry. I realized this was a great way to be creative and spend quality time together. It was instantly gratifying and I was shocked at how fine my first necklace was. I loved making jewelry and wanted to learn more! I knew then I wanted to open a bead store back home in Naperville, Ill., so I could share this incredible beading experience with others.

The next day I met with the shop owner to talk about opening a bead store in my hometown. I knew my husband, David, would be able to help me get the business started. His only comment was, "You've had some crazy ideas, but this one might be valid." The owner agreed to help us with our business and everything fell into place almost immediately. We opened The Place to Bead two months later in early October; it was the first full-service bead store and jewelry design studio in the area. The shop offered premium beads and findings, classes, parties, and jewelry design consultations. I began to take classes to expand my knowledge and skills, and was always searching for unique beads and findings to carry at the store.

During one of my searches, I came across Venetian glass beads and immediately fell in love with their history and high-quality craftsmanship. As I began researching Venetian beads and how to buy them, I realized how important it was to find a dependable source for quality, genuine Venetian glass beads.

I found that source in Susie and Philip Holland, the first to introduce Venetian glass jewelry to the American market in 1976. They offered the best quality and prices in the industry, and I began buying Venetian beads for the store from them without delay.

The Venetian beads were very popular at our store and during a bead buying trip to Tucson, Ariz., in 2004, Phillip jokingly asked us if we wanted to buy ALL their Venetian beads so they could retire. David and I went to dinner to discuss the business opportunity and the next day we told them we would. In May of 2004, Bella Venetian Beads was incorporated and we were off to Italy for ten days with Susie and Philip to meet the

How Beads Are Made

1
The bead maker heats the first glass color (lime) in the flame and winds the molten glass around a hollow copper tube.

2
The bead maker adds the second color (purple) of molten glass to the bead to make a bicolored disk.

3
The molten glass is heated so it can be shaped.

4
A press is used to form the bead into a disk shape.

5
The finished disk is ready to cool and then go to a nitric acid bath to remove the copper tube.

1

bead makers with whom they had been doing business for almost 30 years. During the trip to Venice, David and I spent time getting to know the bead makers, learning about the history of Venetian beads, and visiting glass factories and museums in Murano. We wanted to learn everything so we could continue to educate customers on the history that began hundreds of years ago, while maintaining the integrity of Venetian beads in today's market.

Since 2004, we have more than tripled our original inventory by adding new styles, shapes, and color combinations to the Venetian bead collection, and we proudly exhibit the largest traveling collection of genuine Venetian glass beads at shows from coast to coast each year.

As we continue to educate bead enthusiasts on spotting imitations and explain the centuries-old process for making Venetian glass beads, I've had the pleasure of creating new jewelry designs to showcase these remarkable beads. The inner beauty of Venetian glass—with its bold shapes and diverse combinations of beaming colors—is incredibly adaptable to jewelry design. Venetian beads combine well with many bead types including semiprecious stones, pearls, crystals, metals, or even other glass beads.

Kathy Fox admiring the catch of the day at the marketplace in the Cannaregio sestieri in Venice, Italy.

I find the Venetian culture and history of glassmaking alluring and I am passionate about maintaining the integrity of Venetian glass beads. I've written this book to share the history of Venetian beads and Murano glass, to help keep the trade alive, and to inspire jewelry designers to incorporate these history-infused beads into modern designs.

Others before me have written about the history of Venetian beads and culture. I've resourced the following books to help me accurately recount the history: *Middle Eastern and Venetian Glass Beads* by Augusto Panini (Skira, 2007); *The History of Beads: From 30,000 B.C. to the Present*, Concise Edition by Lois Sherr Dubin (Thames and Hudson, 1995); *Collectible Beads: A Universal Aesthetic* by Robert K. Liu (Ornament, 1995); *The Living Museum*, vol. 65 no. 1, Spring 2003 by Jonathan E. Reyman; and *Venice & the Veneto* by Sylvie Durastanti and Angelo Lomeo with Sonja Bullaty (Abbeville Press, 1998).

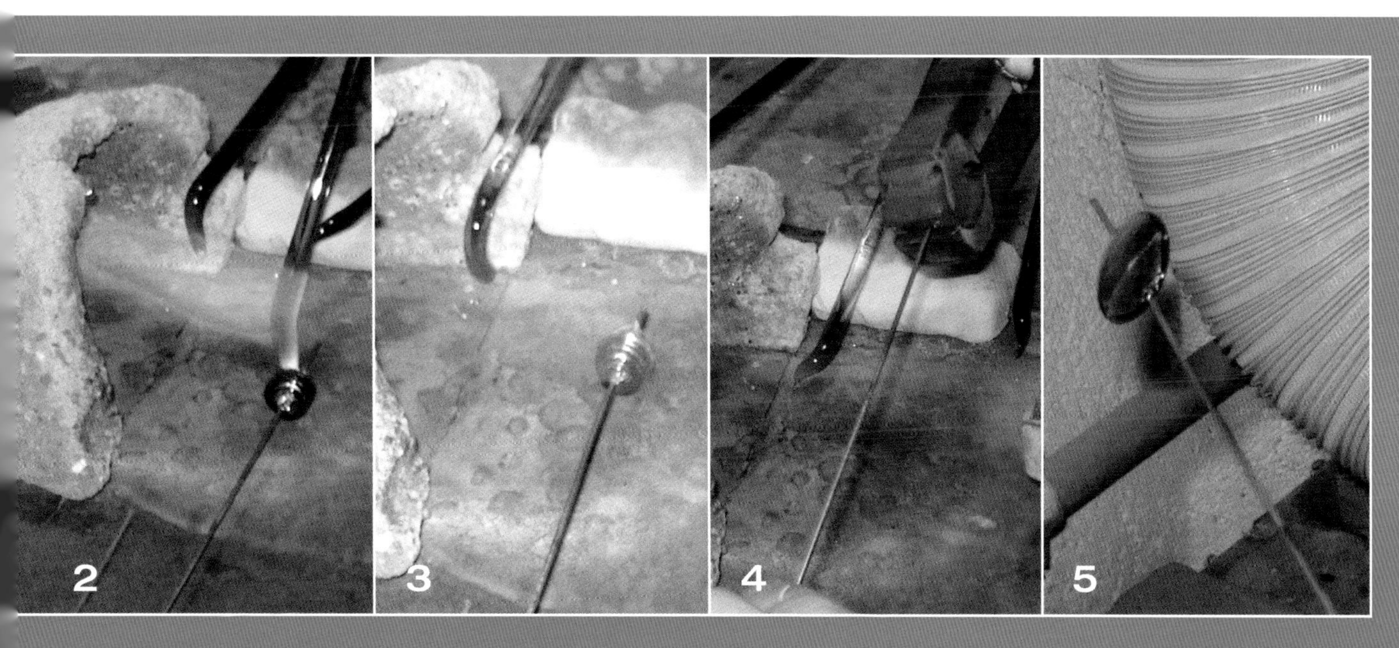

History of Venezia

Venice—one of the most beautiful cities in the world—is a living museum. The Venetian history is remarkable and the city's architecture is awe inspiring. The city, comprised of six sestieri (districts), includes more than 100 small islands and 150 canals in the marshy lagoons of the Adriatic Sea in northeastern Italy. Venice is a city of canals and is also known as the "City of Bridges" or "City of Water"; as a result you will see no automobiles.

Transportation around the city is convenient by water bus or one can travel easily on foot. While it takes only approximately 30 minutes to walk directly from one end to the other, make sure to bring comfortable walking shoes: The maze of alleys will lead you on an adventure of a lifetime and you'll walk for hours, discovering one of the most romantic and beloved cities on earth.

The Grand Canal winds through the middle of Venice and was once the city's main thoroughfare. The palazzo (palaces) of the Grand Canal feature some of the most remarkable architecture of 13th-century Venetian aristocracy. Many are named after distinguished Venetian families and many are now museums, hotels, or shops. One of the most magnificent architectural examples along the Grand Canal is the Ca' d'Oro (house of gold). Built in the 15th century, it's a fine example of Venetian gothic architecture. Today Ca' d'Oro houses the Giorgio Franchetti Art Collection.

The Rialto bridge is in the heart of Venice and has been a busy part of the city for centuries. Until the Accademia bridge was built in 1854, the Rialto bridge was the only way to cross the Grand Canal by foot. This solid stone bridge, begun in 1588, took three years to construct, and replaced a boat bridge from the 12th century. The bridge is built on 12,000 wood pilings and has a span of 157 feet. Today there are many shops around the bridge and it's an excellent spot to find Venetian glass jewelry. The Rialto bridge also offers a breathtaking view of the Grand Canal that is beyond a doubt one of the best scenes to photograph in Venice.

San Marco, one of the most well-known sestiere, is on the southern border of the Grand Canal. San Marco once was the judicial and political center of Venice and today is still considered the heart of Venice. The Piazza San Marco (St. Mark's Square) is a tourist mecca and a familiar scene in many movies.

The Basilica San Marco (St. Mark's Basilica) and Palazzo Ducale (Doge's Palace) are two of the most spectacular buildings in the square. Dating to the 9th century, they feature lavish carvings, majestic statues, and masterful mosaics. Napoleon once described the square as "the most elegant drawing room in Europe," and it was the only square worthy of being labeled a piazza (others were simply called campi, or fields).

1 Grand Canal.

2 Rialto Bridge.

3 Palazzo Contarini del Bovolo.

4 Acqua Alta flood tides.

St. Mark is the patron saint of Venice and the lion is his symbol. Throughout San Marco Square and Venice, visitors will find symbolic winged lions in honor of the saint. Today, the square offers a large number of luxury hotels, restaurants, and shops. Tucked away just west of the Piazza is Palazzo Contarini del Bovolo, which is known for its spectacular spiral staircase, and La Fenice, the city's oldest theatre house, built in 1792.

The Venice Carnevale is one of the world's most famous and extravagant mardi gras events, and it's worth experiencing despite the vast crowds. It was first mentioned in Venice history as a celebration of the victory of Doge Vitale Michiel II in 1162, and masks were first worn in 1268. The festivities lead to Shrove Tuesday and began with the slaughtering of a bull and 12 pigs in the Piazza San Marco, providing an opportunity to indulge before Lent.

Today, Carnevale offers masked balls, costume parades, and abundant entertainment. The elaborate costumes, wigs, masks, dresses, and cloaks can be extremely colorful and glitzy.

On the first Sunday in September in Venice, the Regata Storica takes place on the Grand Canal. The Regata dates to the 13th century and is part of the maritime history, since it was vital to have expert oarsmen. The Regata begins with a colorful ceremonial parade of historical boats. Four rowing races follow: the first for the very young, the second for women, the third for men, and the fourth featuring sporting gondolas.

The buildings of Venice are constructed of wood, stone, and brick that rest on closely spaced 15-foot tall wood pilings that penetrate the clay and sand layers of the lagoons. The wood pilings turn stone-hard because of the salt and the lack of oxygen in sea water, creating a sound foundation for the structures. Many believe that Venice began sinking during the 20th century. Since artican wells in the lagoons were banned in the 1960s, the sinking has slowed, but Venice is still threatened by the high waters of the flood tides, called acqua alta, that occur between autumn and early spring.

The Glassmaking Industry

Glassmaking has existed in Venice since the 8th century and can be directly connected to Roman and Byzantine societies. On the nearby island of Torcello, glass furnaces and fragments of glass dating back to 600–650 CE were discovered at an archeological site.

During the centuries to follow, as the glassmakers of Venice continued to improve their specialized skills in glass production, Venetian glass became prized on trade routes. In fact, bead makers became so skilled that the glass beads made for rosaries imitated rock crystal, aquamarine, and garnet flawlessly. Because of this, in 1284 the Republic of Venice imposed taxes to prevent glass beads from being passed off as precious stones.

By the late 13th century, Venetian glassmakers had perfected their unique and proprietary glassmaking skills. These skills are still used today to make some of the most refined glass in the world. In 1291, the Venetian Republic banned glass furnaces from Venice and moved them to Murano, a small island just north of Venice.

Most historians assume this was done to prevent the fires in the furnaces from burning down the mainly wooden buildings of Venice. However, another possible explanation for the move to Murano was to isolate the master glass-blowers and prevent them from sharing their valuable glassmaking knowledge and secrets with foreigners. As a result of the move to Murano, the glassblowers became like prisoners isolated from outside contact and even condemned to death as traitors if they left.

Murano glassmaking became the leading source of fine glass in Europe during the 15th century.

Mirror production was the main source of trade revenue for the Republic of Venice, but Murano's artisans developed new techniques to create beautiful and intricate pieces. Most of the glass during this period was luxurious, but also practical, including bottles, drinking glasses, window glass, and even reading glasses.

In the 16th century, as European traders now had ties with almost all regions of the world, glass was a novelty. Glass beads were rarer than gems or other precious stones, and the demand for Venetian glass beads was high. To meet this demand, authorities allowed bead making to return to Venice in 1592. Venice soon became the capital of glass bead production and established a monopoly for more than three centuries. From this time, the trade of Venetian glass beads spread throughout the world, and today, Venetian glass beads are still in high demand. In fact, it has been estimated that more than 100,000 styles of beads are produced in Venice for export.

History of Trade Beads

Archeologists tell us beads have been made for more than 30,000 years, and throughout history, they have played a significant role. From the late 1400s though the early 1900s, millions of beads were traded for merchandise in the Americas and Africa, and for this reason the term "trade beads" was coined.

European glass trade beads were mostly from Venice, but Holland, Poland, and Czechoslovakia were also bead sources. European explorers arriving in West Africa in the 15th century saw a wealth of commodities such as gold jewelry, ivory, coconut oil, and incense.

Venetian beads, specifically chevron, millefiori, feather, and seed beads, were made for the African trade and were bartered for these commodities and sadly, also for slaves. It is estimated that 15 million slaves were exchanged for European glass beads and shipped from Africa to the Americas. During these centuries, beads were a primary currency.

Chevron beads, perhaps the most recognizable and collectable trade beads, were created in Murano near the end of the 15th century. Composed from layers of colored glass, a star-like pattern emerges after the ends are ground. Most chevron beads made for export to West Africa and the Americas had layers of red, blue, and white glass.

Seven-layer chevron beads have been found exclusively in the Americas—mainly Peru—and have been attributed to the travels of Christopher Columbus. In Murano today, chevron cane can still be found, but these beads typically have six layers and are made in very limited quantities.

The Picard Trade Bead Museum in California exhibits more than 50,000 beads and ornaments, including chevrons, millefiori, feather, and fiorato beads. John and Ruth Picard are committed to preserving the history of beads traded in Africa over the centuries. They are experts in antique chevron beads and are a great source of information for collectors who want to learn more about vintage and trade beads.

American history has many documented accounts of trade beads use by the European colonists. In fact, when the first colonists arrived in America they gave gifts to the Native Americans including beads. Beads were also used for trade and over time, Venetian glass beads became very popular with Native Americans; they were used to embellish clothing and other objects.

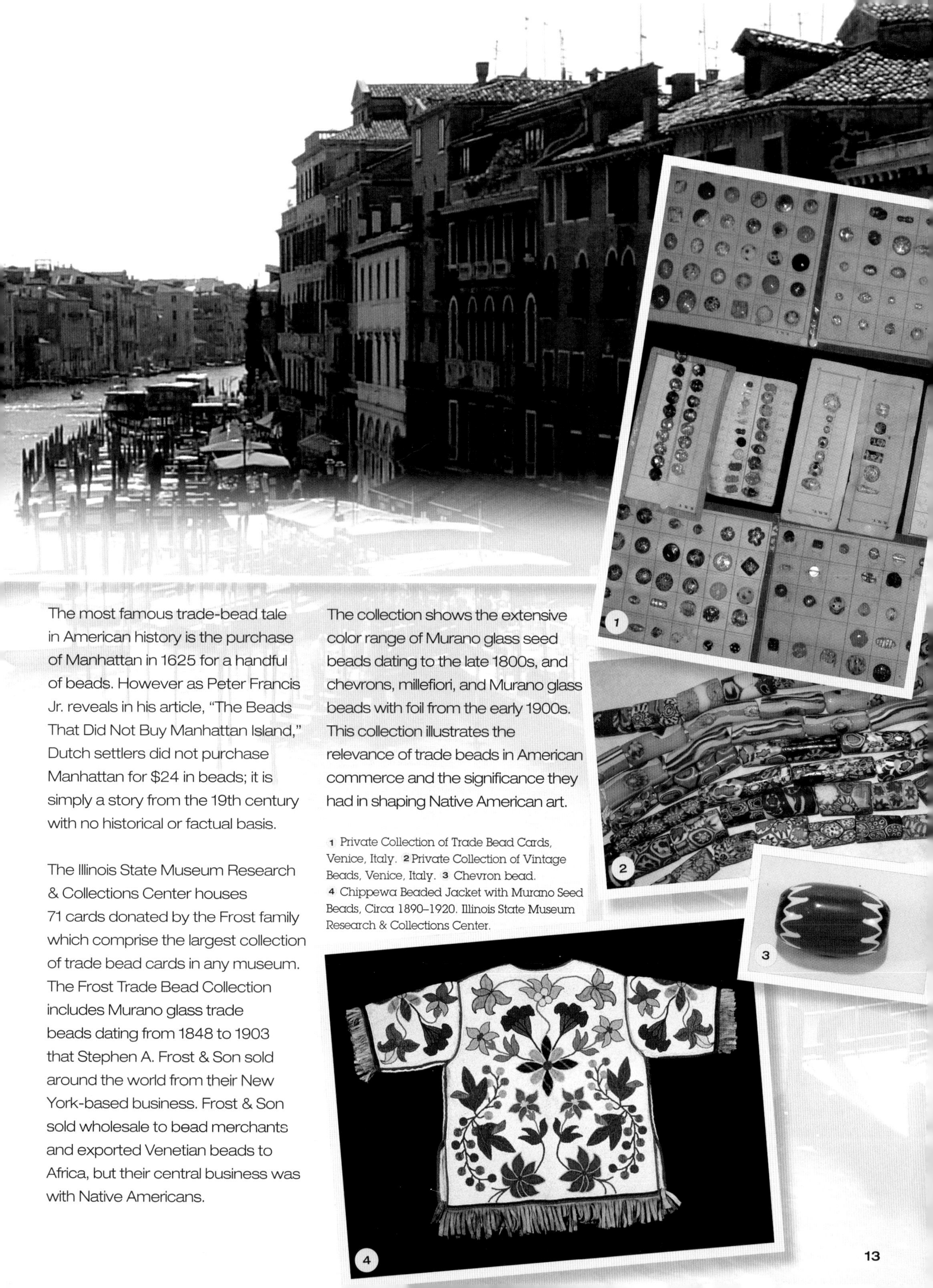

The most famous trade-bead tale in American history is the purchase of Manhattan in 1625 for a handful of beads. However as Peter Francis Jr. reveals in his article, "The Beads That Did Not Buy Manhattan Island," Dutch settlers did not purchase Manhattan for $24 in beads; it is simply a story from the 19th century with no historical or factual basis.

The Illinois State Museum Research & Collections Center houses 71 cards donated by the Frost family which comprise the largest collection of trade bead cards in any museum. The Frost Trade Bead Collection includes Murano glass trade beads dating from 1848 to 1903 that Stephen A. Frost & Son sold around the world from their New York-based business. Frost & Son sold wholesale to bead merchants and exported Venetian beads to Africa, but their central business was with Native Americans.

The collection shows the extensive color range of Murano glass seed beads dating to the late 1800s, and chevrons, millefiori, and Murano glass beads with foil from the early 1900s. This collection illustrates the relevance of trade beads in American commerce and the significance they had in shaping Native American art.

1 Private Collection of Trade Bead Cards, Venice, Italy. 2 Private Collection of Vintage Beads, Venice, Italy. 3 Chevron bead. 4 Chippewa Beaded Jacket with Murano Seed Beads, Circa 1890–1920. Illinois State Museum Research & Collections Center.

Making Venetian Glass Beads

In the early 16th century, Venetian glass artisans began making wound beads or lamp beads. At first, the beads were manufactured for embellishing religious artifacts, decorating clothes, or making necklaces and rosaries. Beginning in the 13th century, craft guilds were organized and regulated by the government and their skills were treated as property handed down from man to man. Venetian women were allowed to work under very strict guidelines, primarily limited to stringing beads in the conterie (seed bead) factories. Glass masters were mostly men and only through stringent provisions were women allowed in bead production.

Nonetheless, by the 18th century women were depicted in paintings as both bead makers and stringers. During World War II and through the 1960s, women were mainly employed in the Murano factories as stringers, but, as the conterie factories began to close, bead stringing disappeared, and more women started making glass beads. During my first visit to Venice to meet bead makers, I was pleasantly surprised to see that many of today's bead makers are women.

1

There are three general types of glass beads: lamp, mosaic, and drawn cane beads. The bead makers in Murano included all three techniques in their production over the centuries.

Lamp or wound beads are beads made from canes that are heated and reheated by a lamp with air created by bellows. Years ago the lamps were fuelled by oil, but in 1842 the lamps converted to gas. The molten glass is wound around a mandrel coated with a releasing agent to prevent the bead from sticking. The beads are normally decorated on the surface by further lampwork with avventurina, colored glass, or foil. Avventurina is a shiny coppery looking substance that means "by chance". It was invented by Vincenzo Miotti in 1625 by chance and has been used in many Murano glass gift items, as well as beads since its discovery. (Most present-day Venetian glass beads are made on a hollow copper wire and will not have any releasing agent in the hole.)

Mosaic cane beads are beads made by heating murrines—thin slices of multiple-colored canes, set one next to the other and heated together. (Millefiori beads are a type of mosaic bead.) It is common to make pendants and glassware by melting murrines together. The millefiori glass rod is made in the same manner as the chevron rod with multicolored layers of glass. The rod is then sliced to make small thin slices, called murrines. The millefiori bead begins as a layer of molten glass that is then covered with murrines. As the flame softens the murrines, the bead maker molds the bead into the desired shape, which joins the murrines together. Millefiori beads are vibrant in color and are made in many different shapes.

1 A female bead artist. 2 Making a two-color lampworked bead. 3 Glass rod stockroom, Murano. 4 A bead maker using murrines to make millefiori beads. 5 Venetian beads slowly cooling in insulation. 6 Acid bath.

Drawn cane beads are beads made with different colored canes that are layered in circle, star, or flower shapes. The canes are immersed in the desired molten glass color and then pressed into a mold to form the shape. This process is repeated, and the bead maker draws the hot glass until the desired number of layers is reached. The large tube of glass is then pulled or drawn in opposite directions stretching up to 50 meters. Afterwards, the cane is cut into beads and the corners are rounded to create a smooth finish.

Venetian beads are wound around a hollow copper wire and when the bead is finished, it is then placed in insulation to cool slowly. Slow cooling helps prevent breakage and will provide heirloom-quality beads. After the bead has cooled, the copper wire is cut and the bead is dipped in nitric acid to dissolve the copper wire. This technique was developed by the Moretti family in 1935, so the hole of the bead would be thinner and crystal clear. Because the hole is thinner and there is no white powder left in the holes from a releasing agent, the beads are much more suited for knotting necklaces. This is now considered the standard practice for all bead makers in Murano and Venice.

Effetre glass, made in Murano, is commonly used to make modern Venetian glass beads. Effetre is a soda-lime based glass with a lower melting temperature than other glasses. When the glass is removed from the flame, bead makers have more time to work to make intricate and delicate designs. The glassmakers in Murano have closely guarded the secret recipes and procedures for making glass rods, and handed them down from generation to generation. The very strict quality standards and raw materials used in Effetre glass are what have helped produce a modern Venetian glass bead that has unparalleled quality and color.

Unlike other art forms, such as oil paintings or tapestries, glass is remarkable in that it maintains its color for hundreds or even thousands of years.

TRADITIONAL *Venetian Glass Beads*

Today's Venetian glass beads are made using the same centuries-old techniques handed down from generation to generation. Traditional styles of Venetian glass beads include millefiori (mosaic), fiorato, feather, chevron, and conterie (seed beads). These beads are a constant reminder of the Venetians' superior bead-making craftsmanship in years past, as well as the significant, historical role they played in the European trade cycle.

Bella Vita
necklace & earrings

Fiorato means decorated with flowers. This very romantic and charming Venetian bead, also known as the wedding cake bead, requires great skill from the bead maker to make the fine flower detailing. A molten ball of glass is formed in the desired base color, a central strip and tiny threads, or stringers, of avventurina are added to the bead, and decoration continues with threads and spots of both avventurina and other colors. Finally, the bead maker uses white and pink stringers to make several small roses. The fiorato remains a classic Venetian bead today. This necklace features a beautiful vintage Venetian clasp, which can also be used as a focal for the necklace.

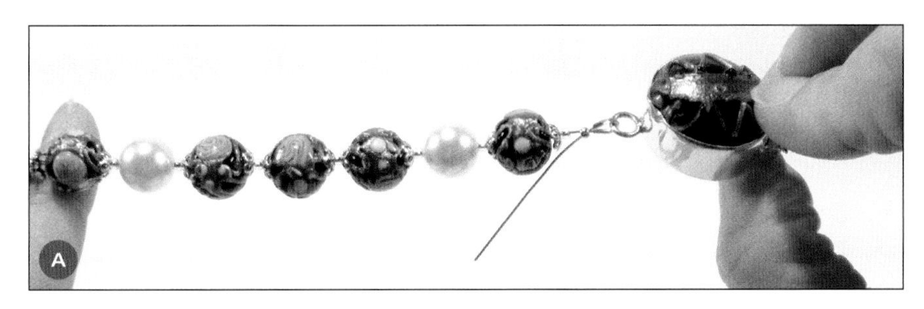

Supplies

necklace

- **26** 12 mm round black fiorato beads
- **9** 10 mm round white crystal pearls
- 11º silver-lined clear seed beads
- **52** 5 mm silver bead caps
- Venetian clasp
- **2** silver wire guards
- **2** size 2 crimp beads
- **2** 4 mm silver crimp covers
- .018 diameter flexible beading wire, 49 strands

earrings

- **2** 14 mm round black fiorato beads
- **2** 10 mm round white crystal pearls
- **4** 5 mm silver bead caps
- **2** 22-gauge sterling silver headpins
- pair French hook earring wires

tools

- chainnose pliers
- micro roundnose pliers
- crimping pliers
- flush soft wire cutter

Necklace

1 String an 11º seed bead, bead cap, Fiorato bead, bead cap, and an 11º.

2 String a pearl and an 11º.

3 String a bead cap, Fiorato, bead cap, and an 11º. Repeat twice.

4 Repeat steps 2 and 3 seven times. Repeat step 2. Repeat step 1.

5 On each end, string a crimp bead, wire guard, and half the clasp. Go back through the crimp bead **A** and crimp both ends (basics). Trim any excess wire. Place crimp covers over the crimp beads **B**.

Earrings

1 On a headpin, string a bead cap, Fiorato bead, bead cap, and pearl **C**.

2 Wire wrap (basics) above the beads and attach an earring wire **D**.

3 Make a second earring.

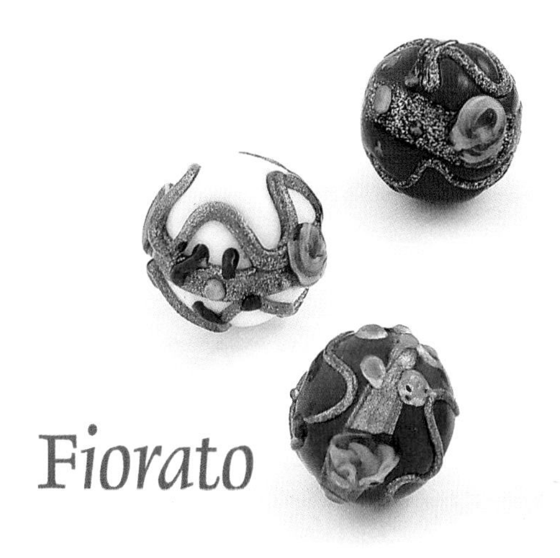

Madonna dell'Orto
rosary

One of the more well-known Venetian beads is the millefiori (mosaic), which literally means a thousand flowers. A traditional Venetian bead style, it adds a splash of color to many jewelry designs.

Early Venetian beads were often used for rosaries, a traditional Catholic devotion to the Virgin Mary. Rosaries are arranged in five decades, a group of 10 beads signaling each time the Hail Mary is to be recited. To separate the decades, an Our Father bead is placed where the Lord's Prayer is to be recited.

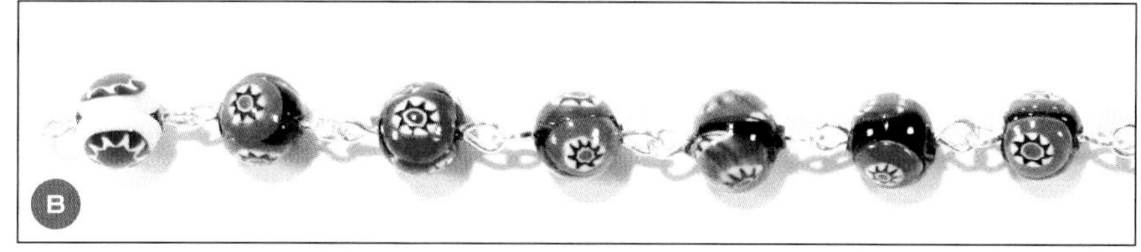

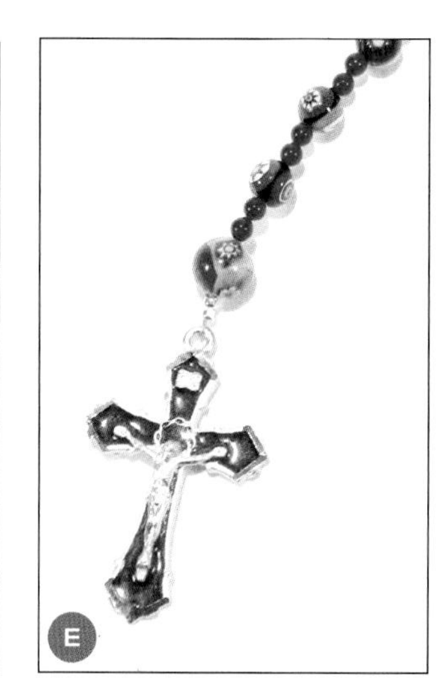

1 Cut a 2-in. piece of wire and make a make a loop at one end (basics). Place a bead on the wire and make a loop on the other end. Repeat until all the millefiori and accent beads have loops on each end **A**.

2 Connect an accent bead and 10 millefiori beads **B**. Repeat four times (50 millefiori beads and five accent beads).

3 Attach the rosary connector to the end beads **C**.

4 Attach an accent bead, three millefiori beads, and an accent bead. Connect the crucifix at the end **D**.

Option: If you do not have the time to make all the loops for the rosary, string the rosary pattern on flexible beading wire using two 4 mm rounds as spacers between each bead. Crimp the ends to the connector and crucifix to finish (basics). This makes a very attractive rosary that is easy enough for even children to complete **E**.

Supplies

- **6** 10 mm beads in accent color
- **53** 8 mm millefiori beads
- rosary crucifix
- rosary connector
- 10 ft. 20-gauge sterling silver round half-hard wire

tools

- chainnose pliers
- micro roundnose pliers
- flush soft wire cutter

Millefiori

Giovanni
leather necklace

The chevron bead, or rosetta, is also known as the "Queen of Venetian Beads" and is the most widely recognized trade bead. At the end of the 15th century, Maria Barovier, who belonged to a family of famous glassmakers, developed the chevron. Presently, chevrons are popular collector items and most often connected with West Africa where they are frequently found.

In modern-day West Africa, chevrons are worn as a sign of prestige during special ceremonies and even buried with the dead. The chevron is considered a masculine Venetian bead and is typically not preferred by women. Authentic Venetian chevrons are becoming harder and harder to find due to the widespread distribution of replicas.

Supplies

- **9** 10 mm oval chevron beads, black
- 6º seed beads, opaque black
- **4** size 1 black crimp beads
- 8 mm sterling silver jump ring
- 6 mm sterling silver jump ring
- **4** sterling silver pinch crimp ends with 3 mm opening
- sterling silver lobster claw clasp
- .018 flexible beading wire, black, 19 strands
- 10 in. of 3 mm diameter black braided leather cord
- G-S Hypo cement

tools

- chainnose pliers
- crimping pliers
- flush soft wire cutter

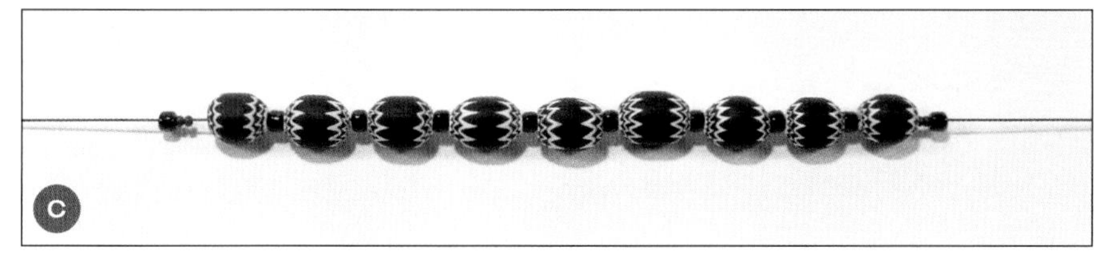

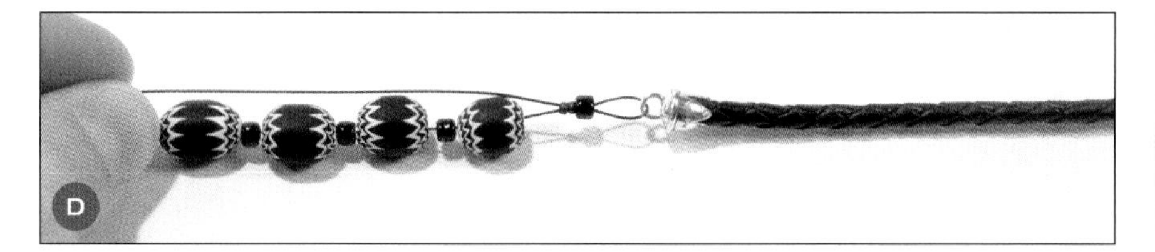

1 For an 18-in. choker, cut two 5-in. pieces of leather. Dab a leather end with glue and insert into a pinch crimp end **A**. Using chainnose pliers, squeeze the prongs of the pinch crimp to grip the leather securely **B**. Repeat on each end of each piece of leather.

2 Cut 9 in. of flexible beading wire. String a 6º seed bead, two crimp beads, and a chevron. Continue alternating 6ºs and chevrons until you've strung nine chevrons. String two crimp beads and a 6º **C**.

3 String one wire end through a crimp end loop. Go back through the 6º and two crimp beads **D**. Crimp the crimp beads (basics) and trim any excess wire **E**. Repeat on the other end.

4 On one end of the necklace, attach an 8 mm jump ring to a crimp end loop. On the other end, use a 6 mm jump ring to attach a lobster claw clasp **F**.

Chevron

Art Nouveau
coil bracelet

The Venetian feather bead is a graceful and stylish bead. Hundreds of years ago, bead makers created this style of feather decoration throughout the bead by trailing lines of molten glass and/or avventurina across the surface. In the early 1900s, when the art nouveau style was popular, the feather bead had its place in many jewelry designs. It is still very common in Venetian jewelry today.

Feather Bead

Bracelet

1 Set up the Coiling Gizmo using the thinner rod. Wrap the 24-gauge vintage bronze wire around the end and over the rod **A**.

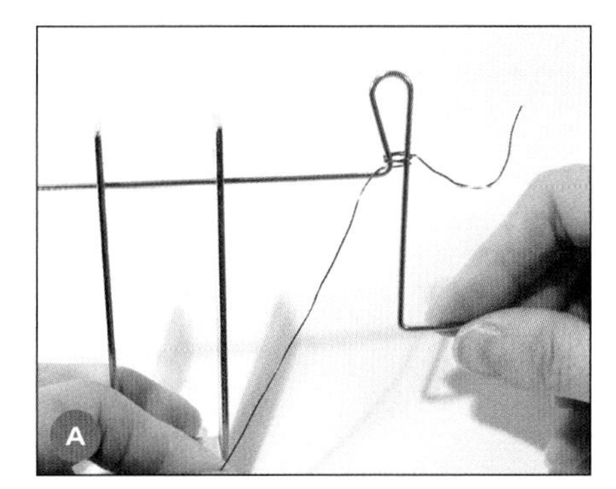

2 Holding the wire against the base of the Coiling Gizmo with your thumb, rotate the coiling rod away from you to begin making the coil. In the beginning, make sure the coils are tight and close to each other. Then push the coils so they are touching the base while rotating to make a nice tight coil **B**.

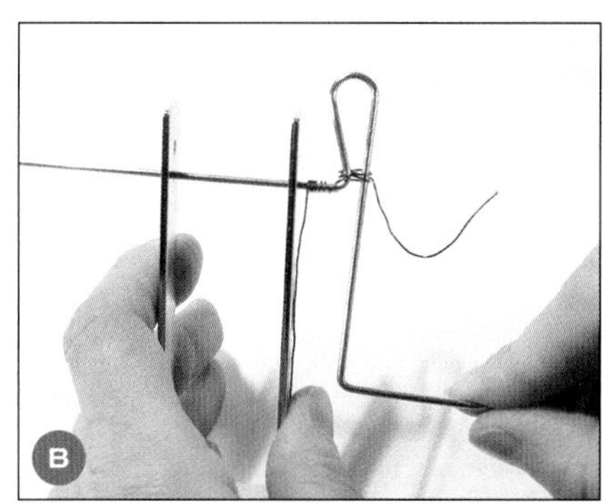

3 Continue to rotate the coiling rod until the coil fills the entire length, approximately 6 in. **C**. Slide the coil off and cut the wire, leaving an 8-in. tail on each end.

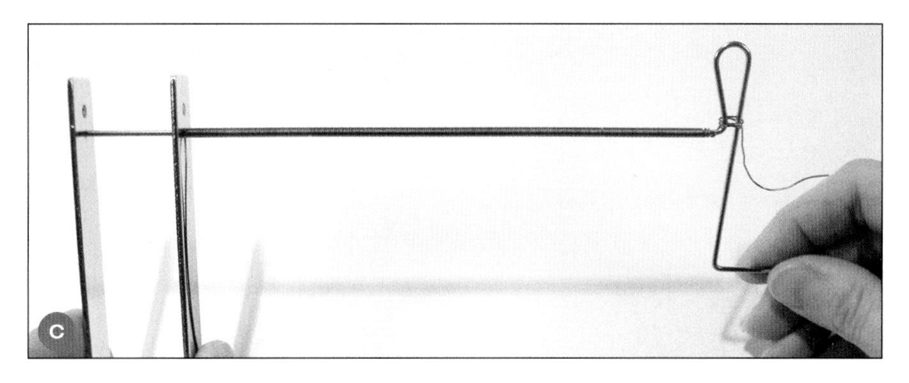

4 Repeat to make two more coils **D**. Set one aside for earrings and for smaller coil beads in the bracelet.

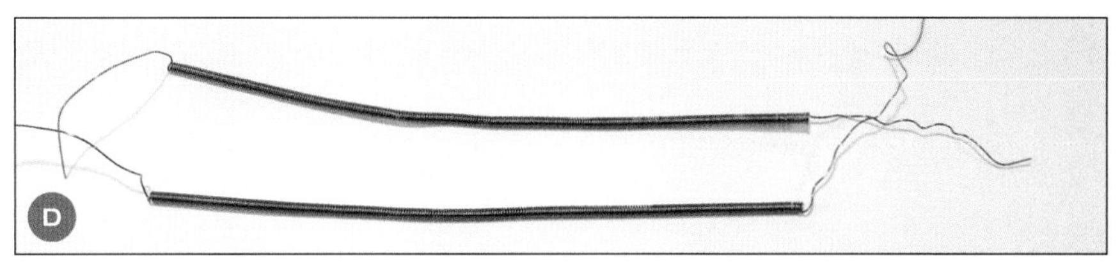

5 Cut the tail from one end of a coil. String the 24-gauge black wire through the coil, leaving the tail at the other end of the coil **E**.

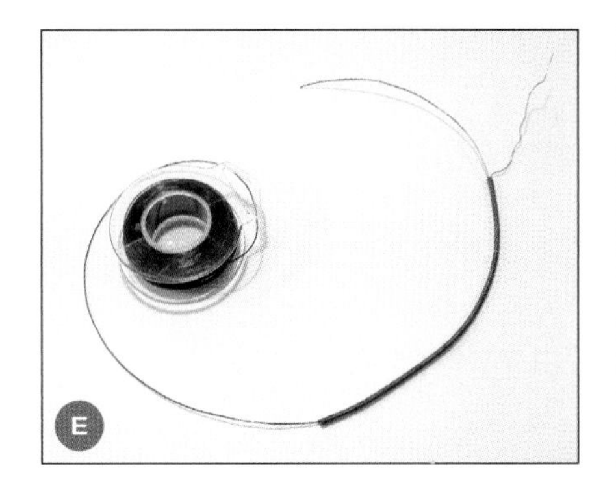

6 Connect the black wire to the end of the coiling rod and rotate to create approximately 1 in. of coil **F**.

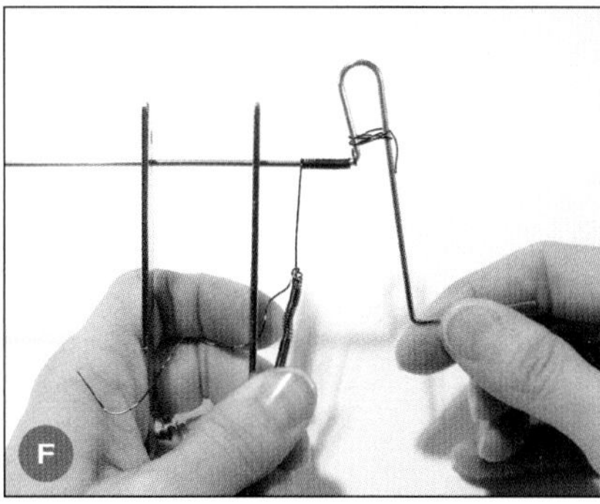

7 Slide the coil to the end and connect the excess wire at the end of the coil to the coiling rod. Slowly begin to rotate the coiling rod away from you to start making the coil wrap around the wire. Make sure to hold the wire and coil close to the base to keep the coil tight **G**.

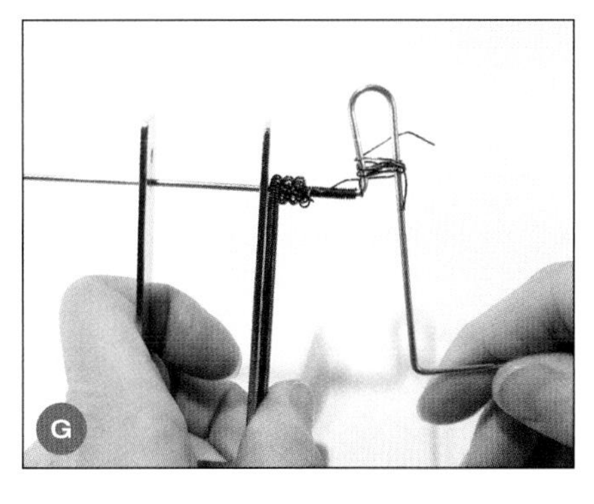

8 After the coil is finished, continue to make another inch of 18-gauge coil at the end. Cut the 18-gauge wire **H**.

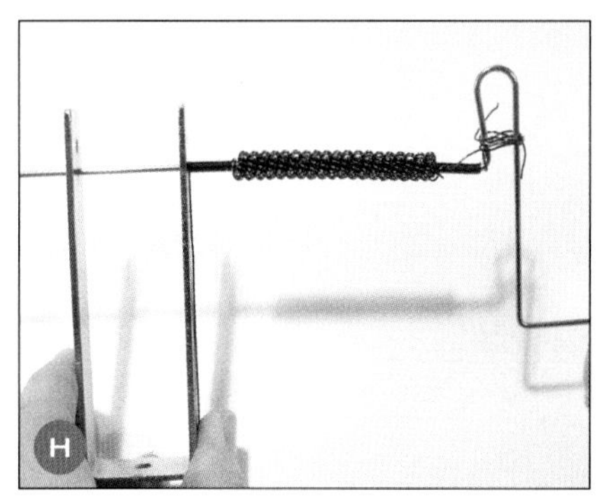

Supplies

bracelet

- 22 mm art nouveau Venetian disk, black/white
- **2** art nouveau nuggets, black/white
- 18-gauge wire spool, vintage bronze
- 18-gauge wire spool, black
- 24-gauge wire spool, vintage bronze
- 24-gauge wire spool, black

earrings

- **2** 22 mm art nouveau disks black/white
- **2** 5 mm brass rounds
- **2** 2-in. brass headpins
- **2** small coil sections reserved from bracelet
- pair brass lever-back earrings

tools

- chainnose pliers
- micro roundnose pliers
- flush soft wire cutter
- Coiling Gizmo

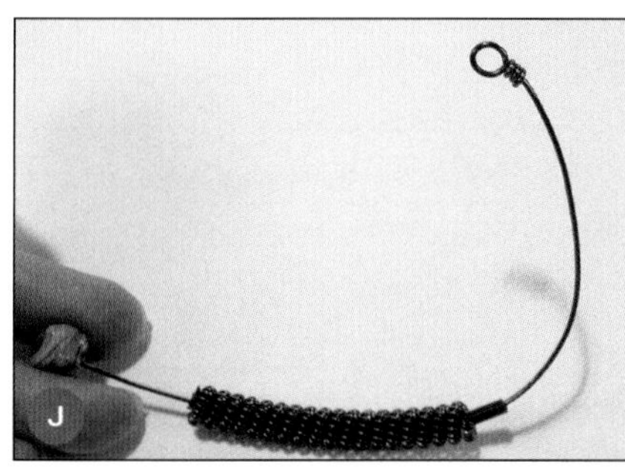

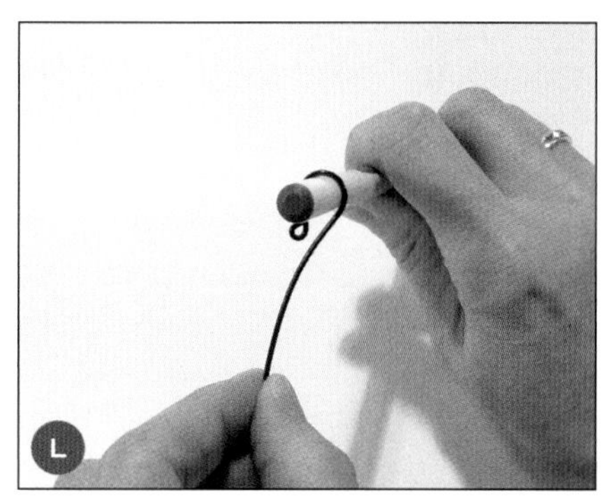

9 Depending on the size of your wrist, cut the finished coil to 2½–3 in., making two equal-length pieces **I**.

10 Cut a 14-in. piece of 18-gauge vintage bronze wire and make a wire wrapped loop at one end (basics), making sure the loop is large enough for the closure to fit. String the first finished coil on the wire **J**.

11 Cut two smaller coils from the coil set aside in step 4 (depending on the bracelet size desired). String the nugget bead, a small coil, 22 mm disk, small coil, nugget, and the large coil piece to complete the bracelet **K**.

12 Wire wrap the end, making a loop (basics). Cut a 5-in. piece of 18-gauge black wire and using the micro round-nose pliers, make a small loop at the end of the black wire. Make sure the loop fits in one of the loops on the bracelet end. Wrap the wire around a ball point pen to make an S-closure **L**.

13 Finish the closure by wire wrapping (basics) it to the bracelet loop **M**.

14 Shape the bracelet if necessary and hook the closure **N**.

Conterie

When bead making began in Murano, glass conterie (seed beads) were one of the first styles produced. Muranese bead makers developed the method for making seed beads from long, drawn, hollow canes of glass that were cut into small tubes. The tubes were reheated and rolled in a mixture of crushed vegetable material to make them smooth.

Seed beads were very popular in Venetian embroidery in the late 13th century. Native Americans decorated articles of clothing with seed beads, and between the two world wars, beaded dresses and accessories were trendy in western countries. The largest seed bead company in Murano, Societa Veneziana per L'Industria delle Conterie, was established in 1898 and employed thousands during the 1920s. It closed its doors in 1992.

Earrings

1 String a disk, coil, and brass round on a headpin **O**.

2 Wire wrap a loop (basics) and attach the earring wire **P**.

3 Make a second earring.

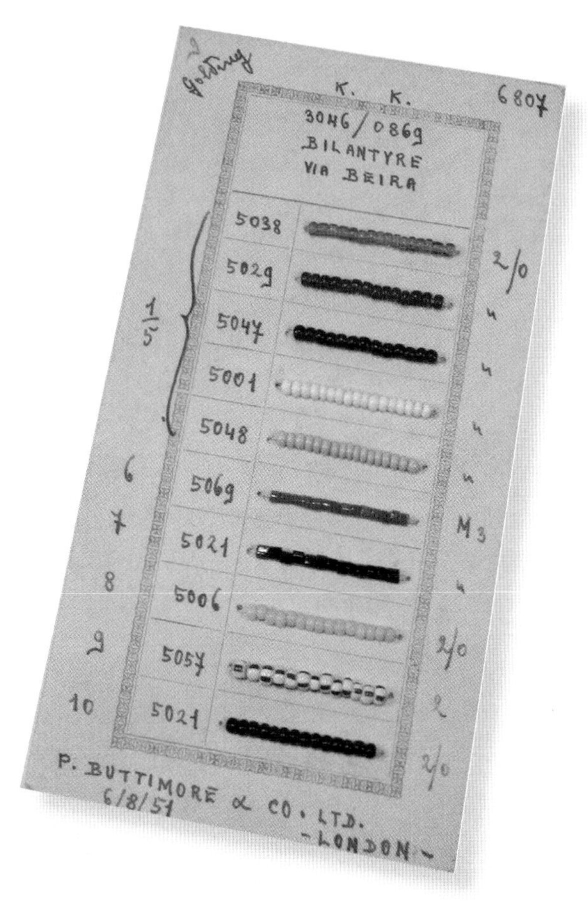

Seed bead trade cards from 1951
courtesy of Nicole Anderson, Venice, Italy.

MODERN *Venetian Glass Beads*

In 1976 Susie and Philip Holland began importing finished Venetian glass jewelry to the United States. Little did they know a bead revolution was on the horizon. At that time, Venetian glass jewelry was made using the traditional bead styles—fiorato, millefiori, and feather beads. As Venetian glass jewelry grew in popularity, the Hollands started exhibiting at jewelry shows and in 1987, exhibited at their first bead show. No other vendor offered Venetian glass jewelry at the show, and the customers were mesmerized with the beauty of the glass beads. Awestruck, they asked where they could buy the beads the jewelry was made from. That night the Hollands cut up their inventory of finished necklaces so they could sell loose Venetian glass beads for the first time, thus—I've been told—starting the rage for Venetian glass beads.

Today, as the appeal of Venetian glass beads continues to grow, so does the variety of bead styles and different bead names. Centuries ago, beads were not given particular names, but they had style numbers or were grouped in generic categories like "fancy beads." As beads grew in popularity in the 1900s, bead makers started creating names for the bead types to help identify and successfully market their personal style of Venetian glass beads. Today there are many different names associated with commonly made Venetian glass beads such as foil, luna, sommerso, gemmato, Missoni, Miro, Klimt, white core, and blown beads. Whether the name is that of a famous artist or simply the Italian word for a type of bead, these names have made Venetian bead styles easier to classify and are now accepted as standard by most bead makers.

Cipriani
bracelet & earrings

Vibrantly colored foil rounds mixed with creamy white pearls create a distinctive finished bracelet and earring set, demonstrating that Venetian beads work in so many combinations.

Supplies

bracelet

- **7** 10 mm foil rounds (rubino/platino, yellow/platino, aqua/platino, pink/oro, lime/platino, aqua/oro, topaz/oro)
- 8 mm foil round (aqua/platino)
- **2** 16-in. strands 5 mm white teardrop pearls (top drilled)
- 2-in. 22-gauge sterling silver headpin
- **2** size 3 silver crimp beads
- **2** 4 mm sterling silver crimp covers
- sterling silver lobster claw clasp
- 1 in. of sterling silver cable chain
- .015 silver-plated flexible beading wire, 19 strands

earrings

- **2** 8 mm foil rounds (aqua/oro)
- **32** 5 mm white teardrop pearls
- **2** size 2 silver crimp beads
- .015 silver-plated flexible beading wire, 19 strands
- pair sterling silver French hook earring wires with crystal

tools

- chainnose pliers
- micro roundnose pliers
- crimping pliers
- flush soft wire cutter

Foil Bead

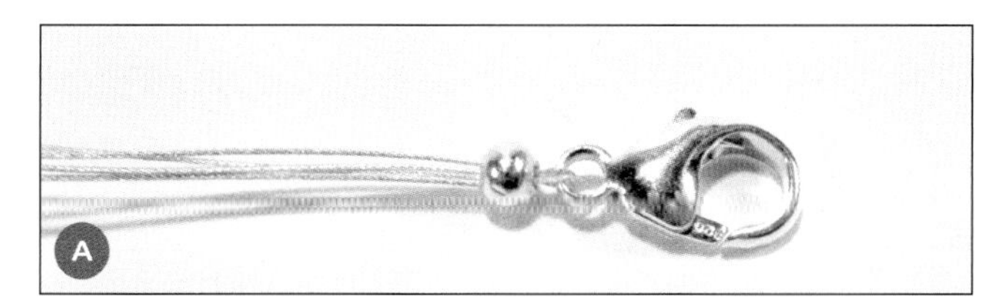

Bracelet

1 Cut two 22-in. pieces of flexible beading wire. Center a lobster claw clasp over the wires. String a crimp bead over all four wire ends and slide it close to the lobster claw clasp. Crimp the crimp bead and close a crimp cover over the crimp **A**.

2 String a 10 mm bead over all four wires. Separate the wires and string four pearls on each wire **B**. String a 10 mm bead to make a pearl cluster **C**.

3 Repeat step 2 until the last 10 mm bead is strung, making sure to keep the pearls in close clusters while stringing.

Note—the bracelet will feel rigid like a bangle.

4 Check to make sure the beads are close together and very little wire is showing. String a crimp bead over all four wires and the through the chain. Go back through the crimp bead and tighten the wires. Crimp (basics), and close a crimp cover over the crimp **D**.

Option: String an 8 mm bead on a headpin and wire wrap (basics) to the last chain link.

Earrings

1 Cut two 6-in. pieces of flexible beading wire. Center an earring wire over the wires. String a crimp bead but do not crimp **E**.

2 Separate the wires and string four pearls on each **F**.

3 String an 8 mm Venetian bead over all four wires **G**.

4 String a crimp bead over all four wires and crimp (basics). Trim the excess wire **H**. Make a second earring.

Venetian Foil Beads

One of the most prevalent Venetian bead styles today is the foil bead. Venetian foil beads have been made throughout the 20th century and were sampled on many of the trade cards in the late 1800s and early 1900s. As they gained popularity in the 1990s, Venetian foil beads became more elaborate. Venetian foil beads are like no others and have superior foiling giving depth to the color of the bead. The foil used in Venetian glass beads can be 24k yellow gold, .999 fine silver, white gold, or a combination of any of these. The difference in quality is noticeable because the foil used is thicker.

Beautiful color combinations can be created by using yellow gold foil with different glass colors. There is a visible distinction between white gold and silver foil: Silver foil is noticeably brighter, and makes the glass color more vivid and dazzling. But since silver foil can also turn black or oxidize, many bead makers prefer using white gold (white gold does not oxidize). Pure silver foil is used today in Venetian glass beads, but there is the occasional black oxidation near the hole of the bead. If silver foil is used in an exposed design, the bead must be processed differently because it cannot be dipped in the nitric acid bath. The Venetian glass foil beads display a richness that no other beads have—the 24k yellow gold is impressive, the pure silver is intense, and the white gold is immaculate.

Venetian beads with exposed white gold: The top set of beads have been dipped in nitric acid and have a coppery color and the beads pictured below were made on a mandrel with releasing powder.

Venetian foil beads are made in all sizes and shapes—from unusual geometric shapes to standard round forms. There are many different methods bead makers follow to shape the beads, and this is why the quality can vary so much from bead to bead. Shaping tools or forms can be used to make very consistent shapes and sizes or the bead maker can work freehand, which tends to create greater variations in uniformity and quality.

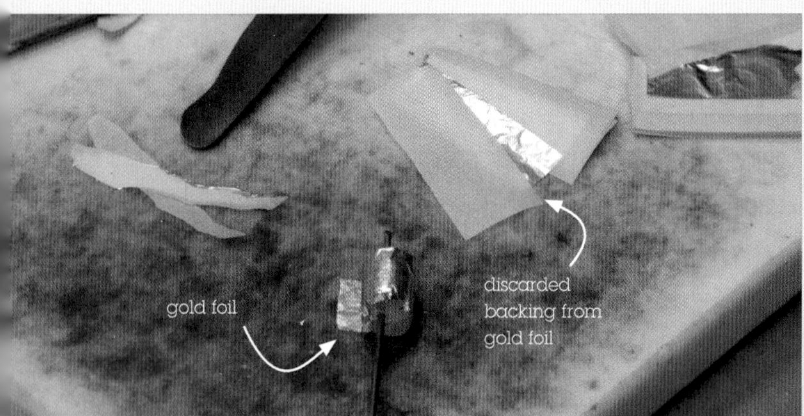

Adding foil as the beads are made.

Ca' d'Oro
necklace & earrings

Most Venetian bead styles have the foiling on the inside, but another technique is to apply the foil to the outside of the bead and leave it exposed. The most common type of exposed foil is 24k yellow gold because there is no reaction when the bead is dipped in nitric acid to remove the copper wire from the hole. White gold can be left exposed, but it occasionally has a slight change of hue, taking on a faint coppery color after the nitric-acid bath. When pure silver foil is left exposed, the bead cannot be dipped in nitric acid, as the silver turns black. To expose pure silver, the bead makers must use a mandrel and a releasing agent. This is one of the few instances where white powder will be in the hole of a genuine Venetian glass bead.

The rich and warm tones of 24k exposed gold mixed with a variety of glass colors create brilliant color combinations for jewelry designs that are sure to dazzle.

Exposed Foils – Yellow Gold and Silver

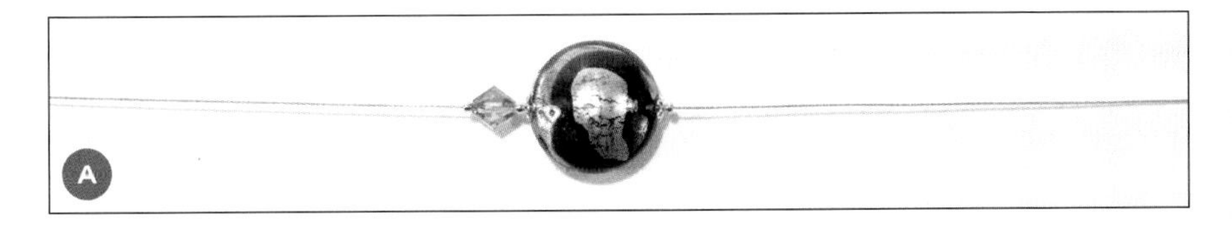

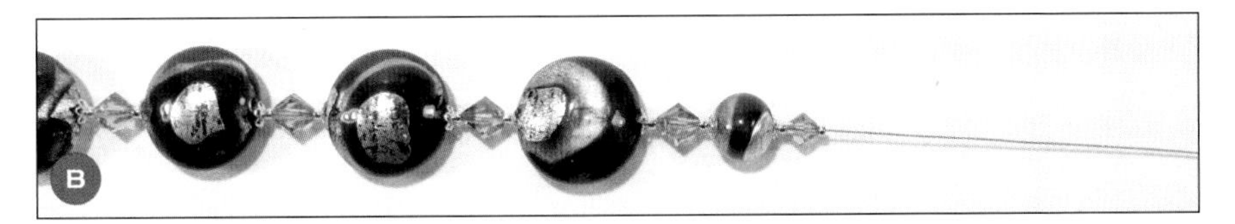

Supplies

necklace

- **5** 25 mm exposed gold disks, aqua/cobalt/oro
- **6** 12 mm exposed gold rounds, aqua/cobalt/oro
- **6** 8 mm crystal bicones, blue zircon
- **6** 6 mm crystal bicones, blue zircon
- 11º gold seed beads
- **22** 5 mm gold bead caps
- **2** gold wire guards
- **4** gold size 2 crimp beads
- **5** mm jump ring
- gold-filled lobster claw clasp
- 14-in. gold-filled hammered long-and-short chain
- flexible beading wire

earrings

- **2** exposed gold 12 mm rounds, aqua/cobalt/oro
- **4** 5 mm gold bead caps
- **2** 2-in. 22-gauge gold-filled headpins
- **2** 3-link chain segments
- **2** gold-filled French hook earring wires

tools

- chainnose pliers
- micro roundnose pliers
- crimping pliers
- flush soft wire cutter

Necklace

1 On a piece of beading wire, string an 11º seed bead, 8 mm bicone, 11º, bead cap, 25 mm disk, bead cap and 11º **A**. Repeat four times.

2 String an 8 mm bicone, 11º, bead cap, 12 mm exposed gold round, bead cap, 11º, 6 mm bicone, and 11º **B**. Repeat five times.

3 Cut two 6-in. pieces of chain. On each end of the beading wire, string two crimp beads, a wire guard, and a chain segment **C**. Crimp the crimp beads (basics) and trim the excess wire.

4 On one chain end, attach a jump ring (basics) and on the other end attach a lobster claw clasp **D**.

Earrings

1 On a headpin string a bead cap, a 12 mm round, a bead cap, and an 11º seed bead **E**.

2 Wire wrap (basics) the beaded dangle to the chain. On the other end, attach the earring wire **F**.

3 Make a second earring.

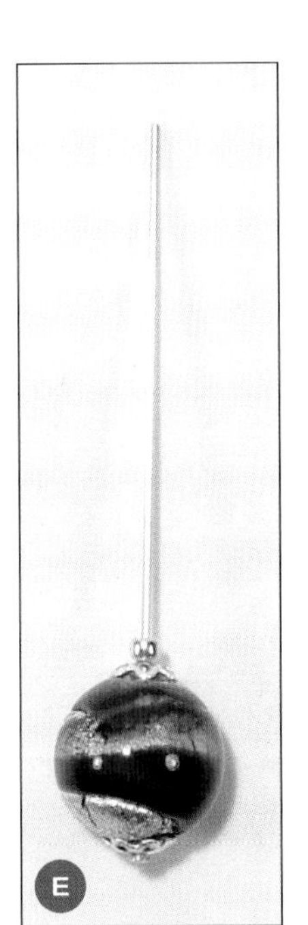

Midnight Skies
necklace & earrings

Luna Bead

The Italian astronomer Galileo wrote the first descriptions of the moon, or luna, after using a telescope in 1609. The variations of light and color in the moon's surface are reflected in the luna bead and are captured by the multiple foils and avventurina used to create it. The luna bead is a breathtaking combination of 24k yellow and white gold, along with avventurina or copper specks, enclosed in translucent colored glass. The result is a sparkling, eye-catching bead resembling Galileo's first descriptions of the moon.

Supplies

necklace

- **13** 20 mm luna disks
- Swarovski crystal 6mm bicones:
  - **14** in a neutral color
  - **14** in an accent color
  - **14** in a matching color
- **26** 4 mm silver bead caps or daisy spacers
- **2** size 4 silver crimp tubes
- sterling silver lobster claw clasp
- 2 in. of sterling silver chain
- .015 silver beading wire, 49 strands

earrings

- **2** 20 mm luna disks
- **2** 6 mm Swarovski crystal bicones
- **2** 4 mm sterling silver bead caps or daisy spacers
- **2** 2-in. 22-gauge sterling silver headpins
- pair sterling silver French hook or post earring findings

tools

- chainnose pliers
- micro roundnose pliers
- crimping pliers
- flush soft wire cutter

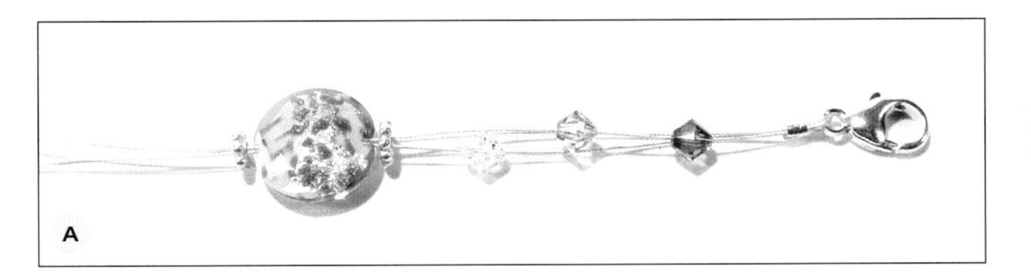
A

B

Necklace

1 Cut three 30-in. pieces of beading wire. String the wires through a crimp tube and a lobster claw clasp. Go back through the crimp tube. Crimp the crimp tube (basics).

2 String a different color bicone on each wire, staggering the placement, and then string all three wires through a 4 mm spacer, the luna disk, and a spacer **A**.

3 Repeat step 2 until all the beads are strung, making sure to push the crystals close together and keep them staggered **B**.

4 String a crimp tube and the chain. Before crimping, place the necklace flat on your work surface and move the beads toward the uncrimped end to space out the crystals and remove any wire gaps. Crimp (basics) and trim any excess wire.

Earrings

1 String a luna disk, daisy spacer, and bicone on a headpin **C**.

2 Wire wrap (basics) above the beads and attach to an earring finding **D**.

3 Make a second earring.

C

D

Danieli

necklace & earrings

Oro Rotto is the Italian name for broken gold. This type of Venetian foil bead has gold foil that appears to be cracked. Although the bead is made in the same manner as foil beads, the bead maker heats the gold foil a little longer to burn away some of the foil and make the cracking effect. Both white and yellow gold are used in this style of bead, and the technique adds an entirely new look to the foil collection. Typically the core of the bead is opaque and the broken gold makes the color jump out in the bead.

Oro Rotto or Cracked Gold Foil Bead

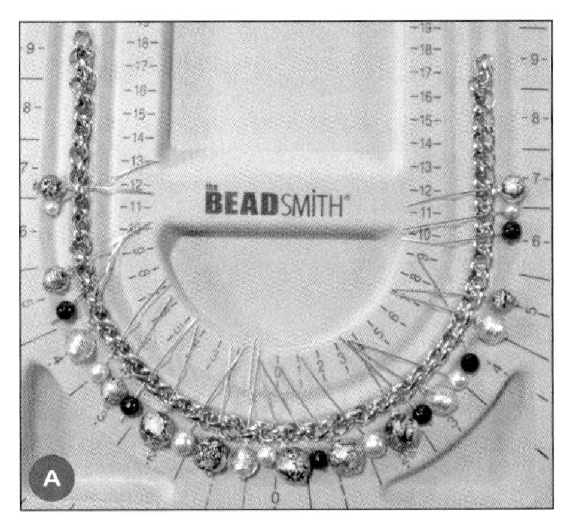

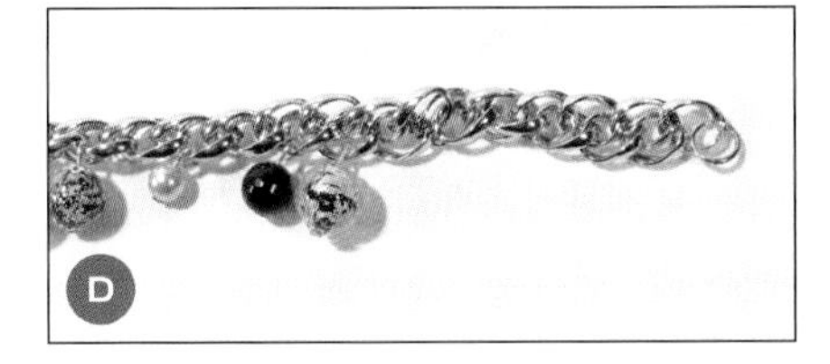

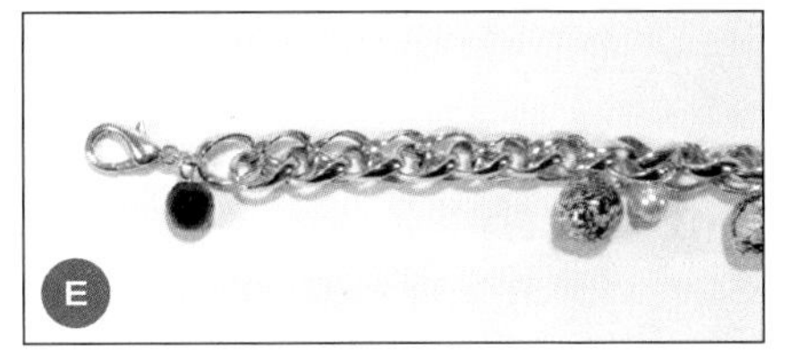

Necklace

1 Lay the chain in the middle channel of the bead design board. String a bead and a bead cap on a headpin. Repeat with all the beads. Arrange the beaded headpins on the chain as desired **A**.

2 Make a plain loop above a bead **B** and attach it to the chain. Repeat to attach all the beads to the chain **C**.

4 Attach a jump ring (basics) to one end of the chain **D**.

5 Attach a jump ring and lobster claw clasp to the other end of the chain. For a finishing touch, add a black onyx dangle to the jump ring **E**.

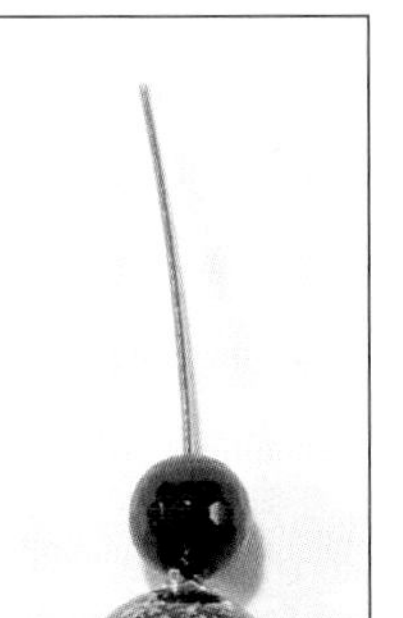

Earrings

1 String a bead cap, a Venetian bead, a bead cap, and an onyx round on a headpin **F**.

2 Make a plain loop above the beads (basics); connect to the earring finding **G**.

3 Make a second earring.

Supplies

necklace

- **5** 14 mm cracked gold black/oro rounds
- **4** 12 mm foil crystal/oro rounds
- **5** 10 mm cracked gold black/oro rounds
- **7** 8 mm black onyx faceted rounds
- crystal gold pearls:
  - **2** 10 mm
  - **3** 8 mm
  - **2** 6 mm
- **28** gold-filled bead caps
- **28** 1½-in. 22-gauge gold-filled headpins
- **2** 5 mm gold-filled jump rings
- gold-filled lobster claw clasp
- 18 in. large-loop gold-filled chain

earrings

- **2** 14 mm cracked gold black/oro rounds
- **2** 8 mm black onyx faceted rounds
- **4** bead caps
- **2** 2-in. 22-gauge gold-filled headpins,
- pair of lever back earring findings

tools

- chainnose pliers
- micro roundnose pliers
- flush soft wire cutter
- bead design board

Lucia
wrap bracelet

Sommerso (submerged) is a style of bead with "floating" colors within layers of glass. The sommerso bead is quite captivating as it contains gold or silver leaf and avventurina in its middle. It begins with a small piece of molten glass wound around copper wire. Next, gold or silver foil and avventurina are applied to the hot glass and completely covered with another layer of transparent glass. The bead is then shaped and the layers form a beautiful bead with color dancing on the inside.

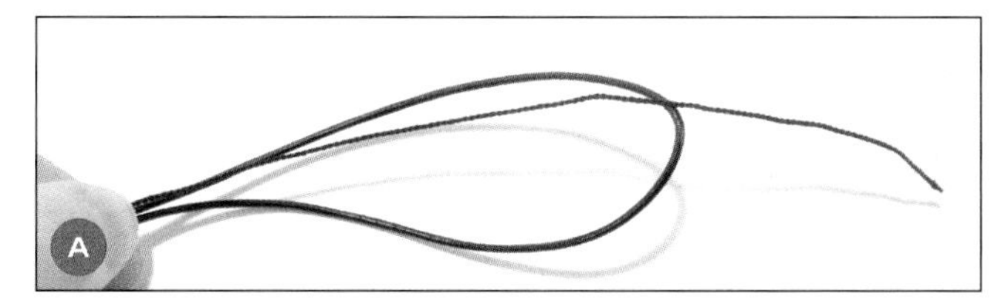

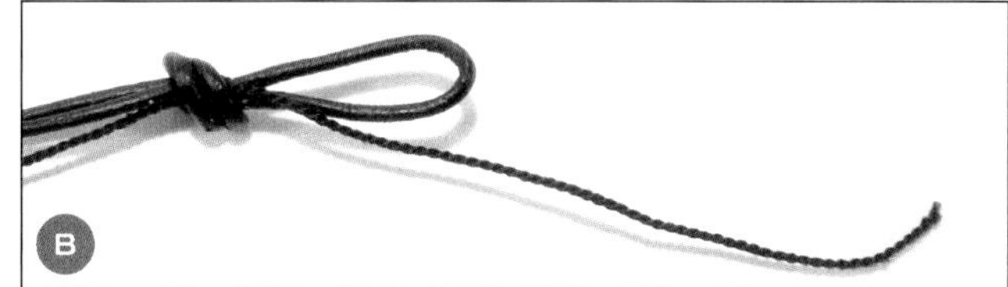

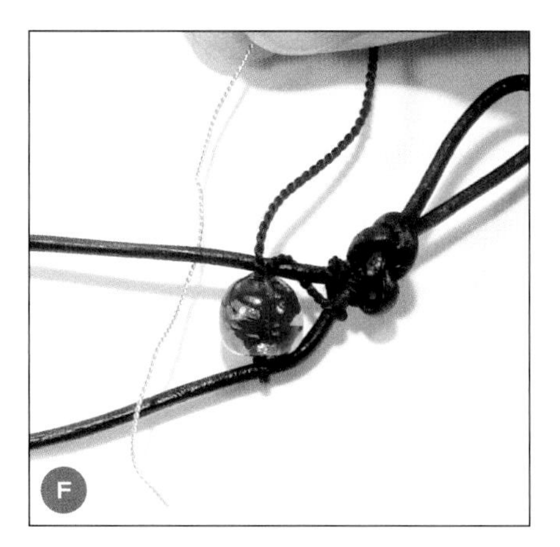

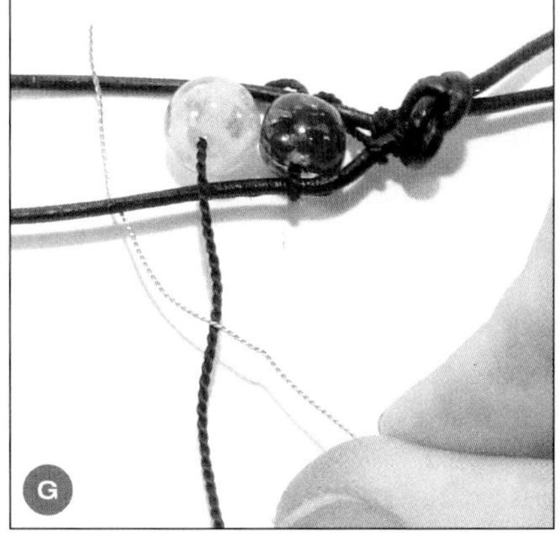

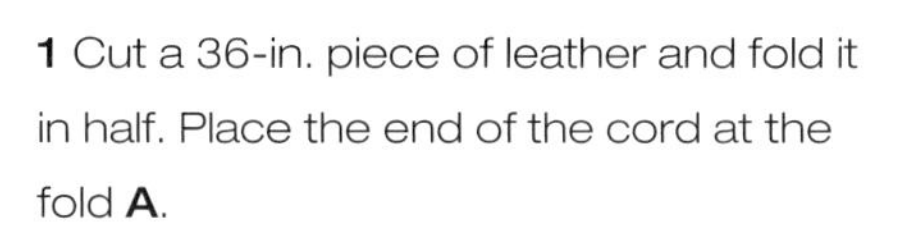

1 Cut a 36-in. piece of leather and fold it in half. Place the end of the cord at the fold **A**.

2 Tie an overhand knot with the leather and the cord to make the loop for the closure **B**. Cut the excess cord from the loop and glue the end to secure it in the knot.

3 Make a knot around one side of the leather with the cord **C**.

Tip—Secure the leather loop by taping it to your work surface or clipping it to a foam board or bead board. This will make it easier to string the beads.

4 Pull the knot in the cord tight up to the knot in the leather at the end. String the needle between the two leather pieces and then over the leather cord at the bottom and under the leather, making a figure-8 **D**.

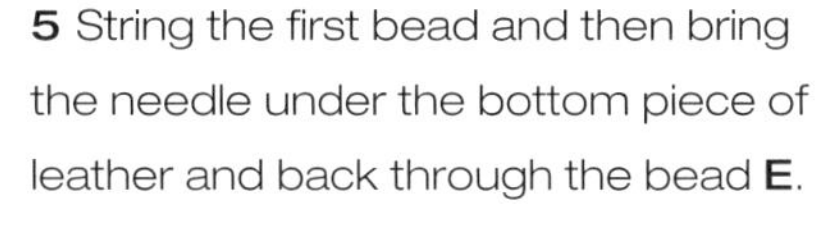

5 String the first bead and then bring the needle under the bottom piece of leather and back through the bead **E**.

6 String the needle under the top piece of leather **F**.

7 String the next bead, bring the needle under the bottom piece of leather, and go back through the bead **G**. Repeat to add the rest of the beads, making figure-8s until the bracelet is the desired length.

8 When the bracelet is the desired length, tie a knot on one of the leather cords **H**.

9 Tie a knot or two, tying the silk cord into the knot again. Make sure the knot is the right size for the loop at the other end. Trim the excess cord and leather and glue the knot to secure it **I**.

Supplies

- **19–22** 8 mm Sommerso rounds (variety of colors)
- 1.5 mm diameter Greek leather cord, black
- silk bead cord, black, size 8 with attached needle
- G-S Hypo cement

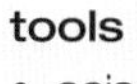

tools

- scissors

Sommerso

Vivaldi
ring

The white core bead is a simple and basic Venetian bead style. The bead starts with a center "core" of white or colored opaque glass, which gives the colored glass that encases it a distinctly lighter look. Although this bead is usually very plain looking, it can be made with multiple colors, stripes, or dots to add contrast, resulting in a very striking and complex appearance. Some white core beads have gold accents and are very intricate and alluring.

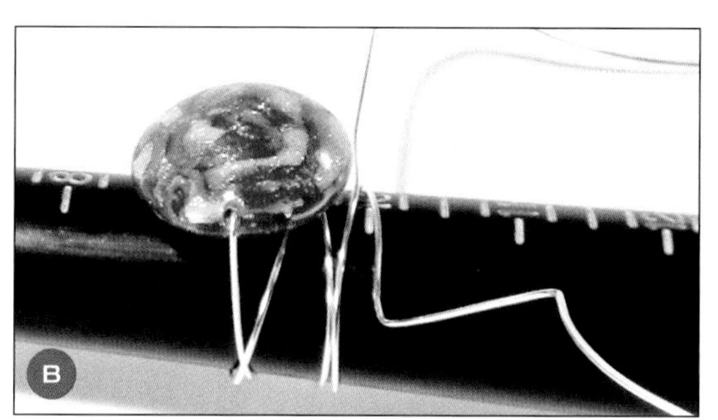

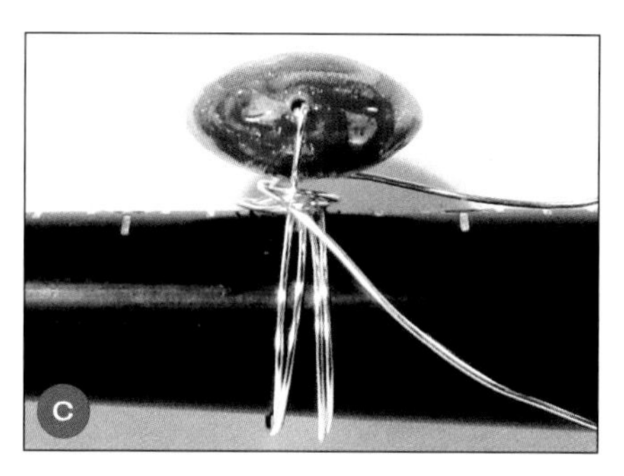

1 Center the bead on the wire and bend the wire down on both sides to hold the bead in place **A**.

2 Measure your finger with the ring sizer and add a half size. Place the wired bead on the ring mandrel on this size. Sit down, and put the ring mandrel between your knees for a secure hold while freeing up both hands. Wrap both wires completely around the mandrel simultaneously three times to make the base **B**.

Tip—Take care to keep the bead on the size desired, as it tends to move up the mandrel and create a smaller size.

4 To make the bezel, wrap the wires simultaneously underneath the bead two or three times, ending with a wire on each side of the bead **C**.

5 Grasp the ring tightly and remove it from the mandrel. Wrap the excess wire through the base of the ring, near the bezel, once on both sides to keep the size of the ring in place **D**.

Tip—Try on the ring at this point to make sure it is a loose fit. If the ring is too small, place it back on the mandrel and unwrap the bezel carefully. Slide the ring down to make it larger and then wrap the bezel again. Be careful to avoid over hardening the wire by rewrapping too much, which will make it brittle and prone to breaking.

6 Wrap the excess wires around each side of the base of the ring, making tight coils to finish off the sides of the ring. For a comfortable fit, do not allow the wraps to extend more than halfway down the side of the ring **E**.

7 Trim any excess wire and use chainnose pliers to tuck the ends under **F**.

Supplies

- 22 mm 24k gold avventurina swirl disk or square
- 20 in. 22-gauge half-hard round sterling silver wire

tools

- chainnose pliers
- flush soft wire cutter
- ring sizer
- ring mandrel

White Core

Rezzonico
necklace & earrings

Gemmato means "full of gems" in Italian. These beads showcase bits of brightly colored translucent or opaque glass called frit. Frit can either be fused inside crystal glass or fused on the outside of beads with exposed gold, giving them a gem-encrusted look. The gemmato style mixes very well with semi-precious stones and is a great complement bead because of its many colors.

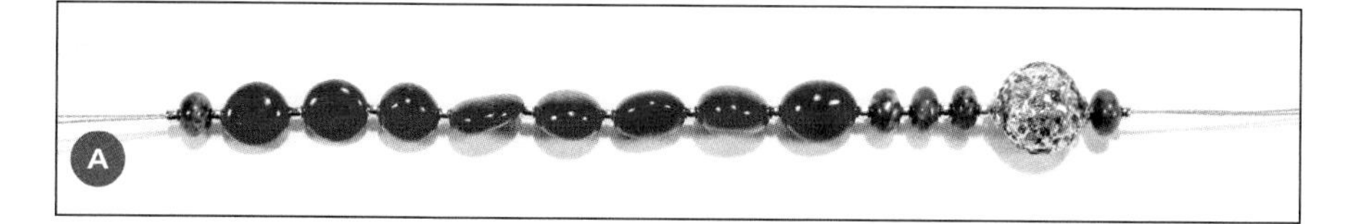

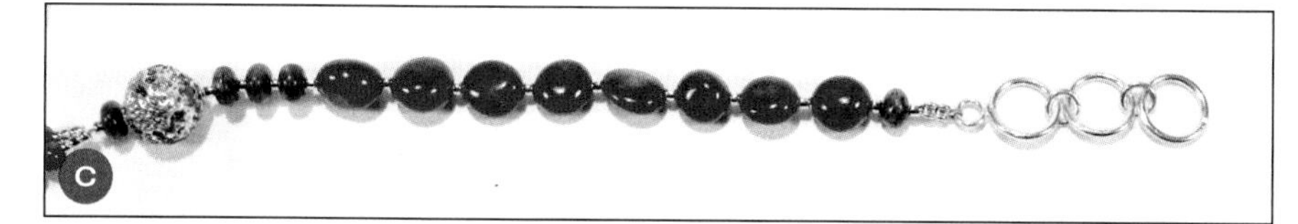

Necklace

1 Cut the beading wire into two 24-in. pieces. Over both wires, string a lapis rondelle, eight red coral nuggets, and three lapis rondelles with an 11º seed bead between each bead.

2 Over both wires, string a bead cap, 12 mm gemmato round, a bead cap, a lapis rondelle, and an 11º **A**.

3 Separate the wires. On one wire string three 11ºs, three red coral 4 mm rounds, an 11º, a 4 mm lapis round, an 11º, a bead cap, an 8 mm gemmato, a bead cap, an 11º, a red coral nugget, an 11º, a red coral nugget, an 11º, a 4 mm lapis round, a bead cap, a gemmato, a bead cap, a 4 mm lapis, an 11º, a red coral nugget, an 11º, and a red coral nugget.

4 String a bead cap, a gemmato flat oval, and a bead cap.

5 String the pattern in step 3 in reverse.

6 On the remaining wire, string three 11ºs, three red coral 4 mm rounds, an 11º, a 4 mm lapis round, an 11º, three red coral 4 mm rounds, a bead cap, an 8 mm gemmato, a bead cap, a red coral nugget, an 11º, a red coral nugget, an 11º, a red coral nugget, an 11º, a 4 mm lapis round, an 11º, a bead cap, a 10 mm gemmato round, and a bead cap.

7 String the pattern in step 6 in reverse on the remaining wire **B**.

8 String both wires through an 11º and string the reverse of the pattern in step 1.

9 On each end, string two crimp beads and half of a clasp. Crimp the beads (basics) and trim the excess wire **C**.

Earrings

1 String a bead cap, 10 mm gemmato round, a bead cap, and a 4 mm red coral round on a headpin **D**.

2 Wire wrap (basics) above the beads and attach an earring wire **E**.

3 Make a second earring.

Supplies

necklace
- 15 x 30 mm gemmato exposed gold flat oval
- **2** 12 mm gemmato exposed gold rounds
- **3** 10 mm gemmato exposed gold rounds
- **4** 8 mm gemmato exposed gold rounds
- 16-in. strand 8 mm red coral smooth nuggets
- **10** 6 mm lapis lazuli rondelles
- **2** 6 mm lapis lazuli rounds
- **8** 4 mm lapis lazuli rounds
- **18** 4 mm red coral rounds
- 11º seed beads, gold
- **20** 5 mm bead caps
- **4** gold size 2 crimp beads
- gold-filled adjustable toggle clasp with three loops
- .013 flexible beading wire, 49 strands

earrings
- **2** 10 mm gemmato exposed gold rounds
- **2** 4 mm red coral rounds
- **4** 5 mm gold bead caps
- **2** 2-in. 22-gauge gold-filled headpins
- **2** gold-filled French hook earring wires

tools
- chainnose pliers
- micro roundnose pliers
- crimping pliers
- flush soft wire cutter

Gemmato

Golden Mosaic
necklace & earrings

Klimt beads are rich in color and detail, as is the work of the artist they are named for. Known for prominent gold leafing, mosaic-like details, and Byzantine influences, Gustav Klimt's work transcends time. This necklace showcases Klimt Venetian beads front and center; a gentle frame of accents finishes the presentation.

A

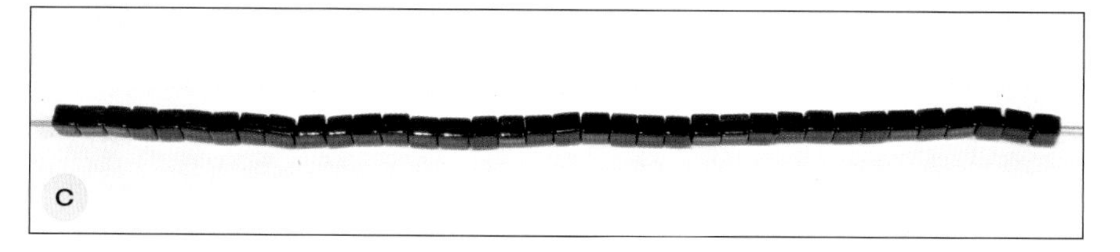

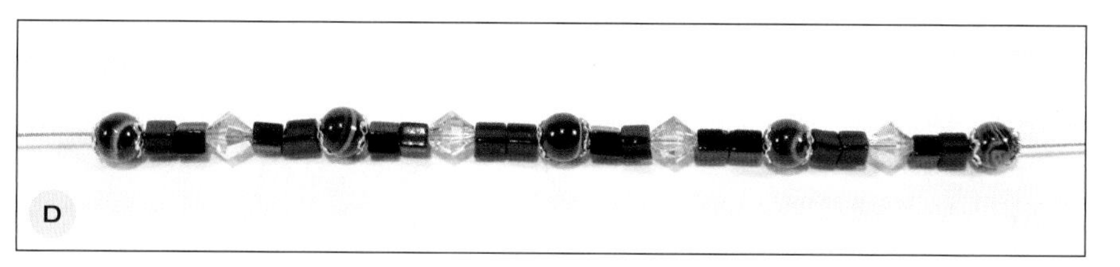

Necklace

1 Cut the beading wire into a 23-in., a 20-in., and a 18-in. length. On the 23-in. wire, string nine 6 mm sardonyx rounds and nine 8 mm sardonyx rounds **A**.

2 String a bead cap, a Klimt bead, a bead cap, and an 8 mm sardonyx following this order for the Klimt beads: 10 mm round, square, 17 mm disk, 22 mm disk, flat oval, 22 mm disk, 17 mm disk, 10 mm round **B**.

3 String nine 6 mm sardonyx rounds and nine 8 mm sardonyx rounds.

4 On the 20-in. wire, string 36 4 mm cube beads **C**.

5 String a 6 mm sardonyx round with bead caps, two cube beads, a crystal gold crystal, and two cube beads. Repeat three times. String a 6 mm sardonyx round with bead caps **D**. String 46 4 mm cube beads.

Supplies

necklace

- 25 x 20 mm Klimt exposed gold millefiori flat oval
- **2** 22 mm Klimt exposed gold millefiori disks
- **2** 17 mm Klimt exposed gold millefiori disks
- 14 mm Klimt exposed gold millefiori square
- **2** 10 mm Klimt exposed gold rounds
- 8-in. strand 8 mm sardonyx rounds
- 8-in. strand 6 mm sardonyx rounds
- **8** 6 mm Swarovski crystal bicones, crystal golden
- **32** 5 mm gold bead caps
- 6º seed beads, black
- 4 mm cube beads, black
- **2** gold triple-strand extenders
- copper enamel toggle, red
- 1-in. gold-filled extender chain
- **2** 6 mm gold-filled jump rings
- 10 mm gold-filled jump ring
- .018 wire flexible beading wire, 49 strands

earrings

- **2** 10 mm Klimt exposed gold rounds
- **2** 6 mm sardonyx rounds
- **4** 5 mm gold bead caps
- **2** 2-in. 22-gauge gold-filled headpins
- pair gold-filled French hook earring wires

tools

- chainnose pliers
- micro roundnose pliers
- crimping pliers
- flush soft wire cutter

Klimt

6 On the 18-in. wire, string 41 6º seed beads **E**. String two 4 mm cube beads, a 6 mm bicone, two 4 mm cube beads, and a 6 mm sardonyx round with bead caps. Repeat twice. String two 4 mm cube beads, a 6 mm crystal, and two 4 mm cube beads **F**. String 41 6º seed beads.

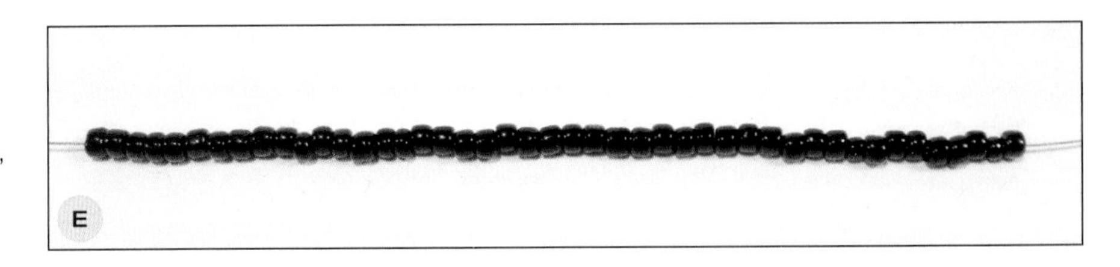

7 Lay the strands flat on the working surface from longest to shortest. String two crimp beads and a connector loop to each wire and repeat on the other end. Go back through the crimp beads and a few more beads. Check the fit and adjust if necessary **G**.

8 Crimp (basics) the beads and trim the wires.

9 Use a 6 mm jump ring (basics) to connect the toggle loop to one end **H**. Use a jump ring to connect the extender chain to the connector. Use a 10 mm jump ring to attach the toggle bar **I**.

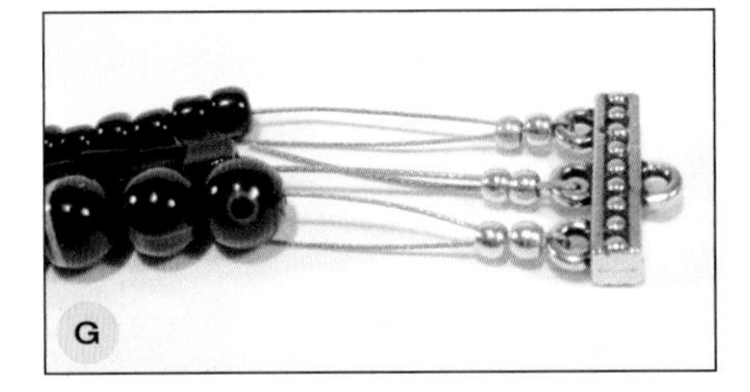

Earrings

1 String a bead cap, a 10 mm Klimt round, a bead cap and a 6 mm sardonyx round on a headpin **J**.

2 Wire wrap (basics) and attach to the earring wire **K**.

3 Make a second earring.

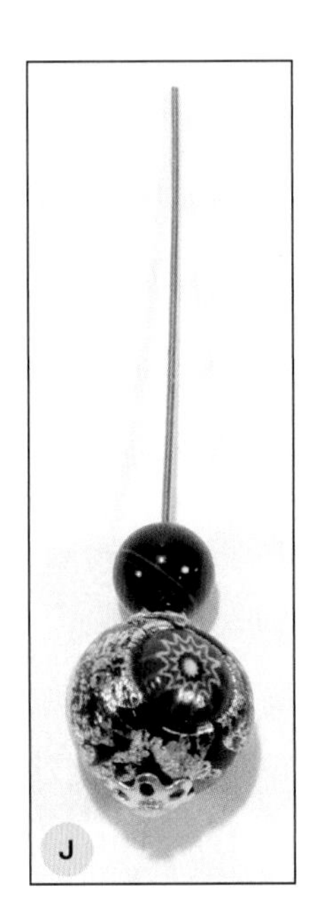

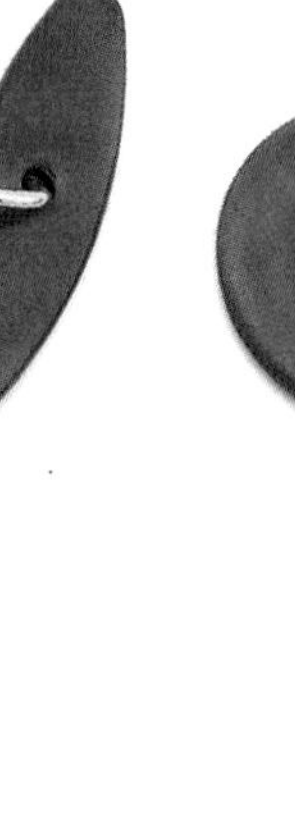

Missoni, Miro, and Klimt

Missoni, Miro, and Klimt are Venetian glass bead styles named after famous artists. Each bead is designed with the artist's style in mind, and the resulting bead styles are widely used by bead makers today.

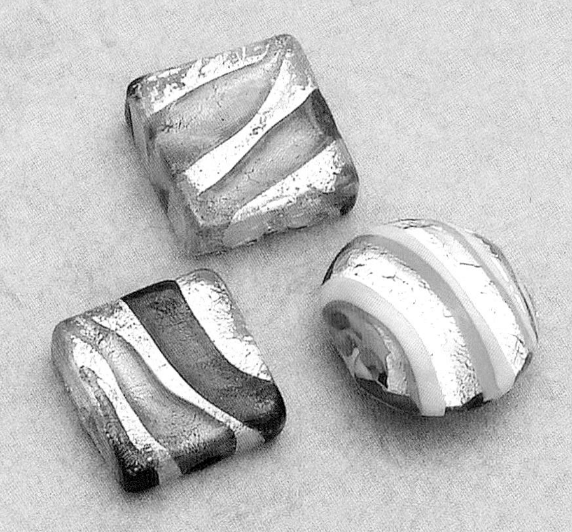

Ottavio Missoni, a popular Italian designer, was famous for incorporating stripes into his designs; a colorfully striped Venetian glass bead is named after him.

Miro beads are inspired by the famous Spanish painter Joan Miró, who expressed his distinguishable abstract style with the use of bold, often distorted forms and brilliant colors.

Artist Gustov Klimt was the inspiration for the Klimt bead, a mix of art nouveau styling and gold leaf details. These Venetian beads incorporate 24k yellow or white gold and glass frit. Some styles incorporate millefiori for even more color.

Acqua Alta
necklace & earrings

Watching a bead maker make a blown glass bead is amazing and captivating. Drawing on traditions from centuries ago, the master bead makers at the furnaces on Murano make these hollow beads by blowing into hot glass rods. The blower continues to reheat the glass in flames upwards of 1600° F, heating and blowing to the desired shape for the hollow beads. It is very common for the blown beads to have variations in both size and shape because of how they are made. Sadly, this type of bead is commonly imitated, making the genuine Venetian blown beads harder and harder to find. Murano glass blown beads are surprisingly strong and typically will even bounce without breaking (unlike imitations which can easily break).

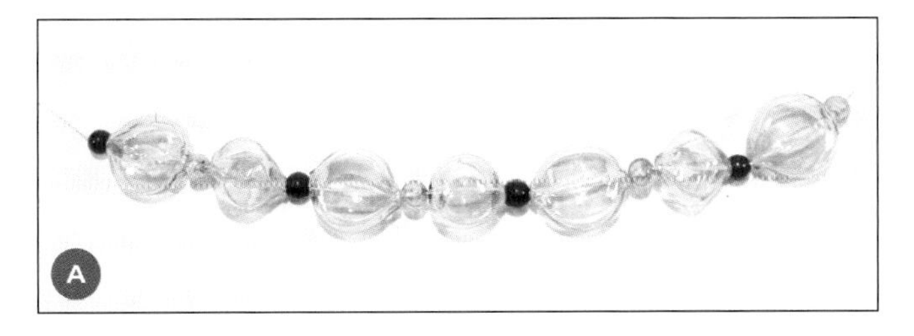

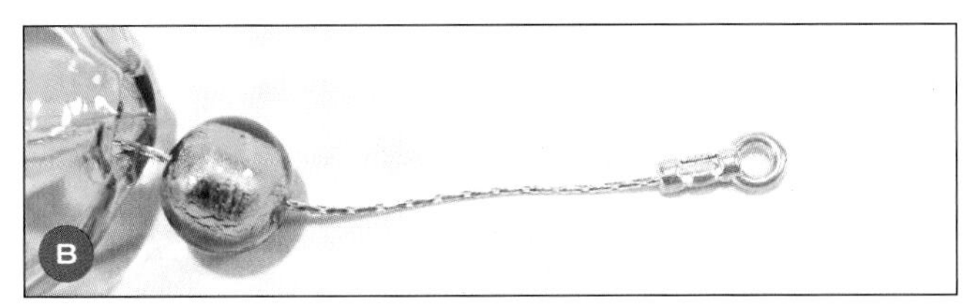

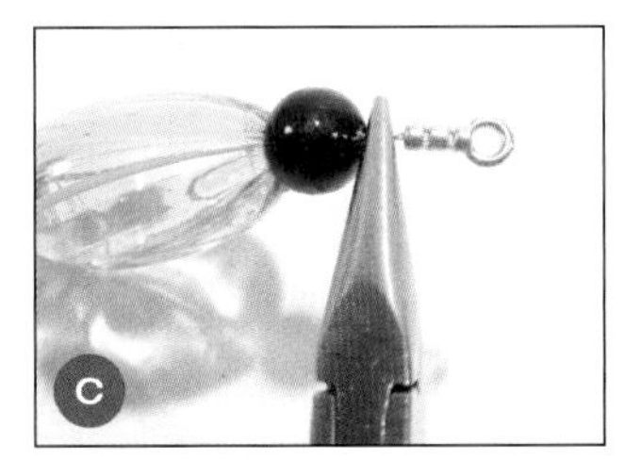

Necklace

1 On the bead chain, string an 8 mm cobalt round, flat round blown bead, 8 mm aqua round, and round blown bead. Repeat twice. String a blown flat round and an 8 mm aqua round. Center the beads on the chain **A**.

2 Place a bead chain crimp end on one end. Use crimping pliers to crimp the middle section (basics). Make sure there is no chain in the loop at the end of the bead chain crimp **B**.

3 Slide the beads to the crimped end and trim the chain to about 8 mm. Use chainnose pliers to hold the chain as close to the beads as possible and slide a bead chain crimp end on the chain **C**. Crimp the chain crimp end in the middle.

4 Attach a 6 mm jump ring to each crimp end. Cut the silk cord into two 12-in. pieces. On each end, string a piece through the jump ring and center **D**.

Supplies

necklace

- **4** blown flat round beads, aqua
- **3** blown round beads, aqua
- **4** 8 mm foil rounds, aqua/platino
- **4** 8 mm foil rounds, cobalt/platino
- **2** Bali silver 5 mm tubes with 5 mm holes
- **4** 6 mm sterling silver jump rings
- 24-in. 5 mm wide silk cord, navy blue
- **2** 12 mm C-crimp cord ends, silver
- **2** sterling silver bead chain crimp ends
- 12-in. sterling silver 1 mm bead chain
- 1½-in. sterling silver chain extender
- sterling silver lobster claw clasp
- G-S Hypo cement

earrings

- **2** blown flat round beads, aqua
- **2** 8 mm foil rounds, aqua/platino
- **2** 8 mm foil rounds, cobalt/platino
- 5-in. beading chain
- **2** bead chain crimp ends
- **2** size 1 crimp tubes silver
- pair sterling silver French hook earring wires with crystal accent

tools

- chainnose pliers
- crimping pliers
- flush soft wire cutter

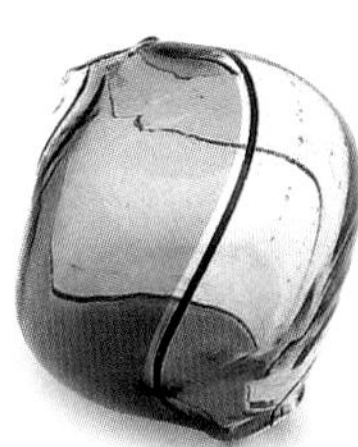

A store window full of imitation Murano glass gifts—notice the low prices.

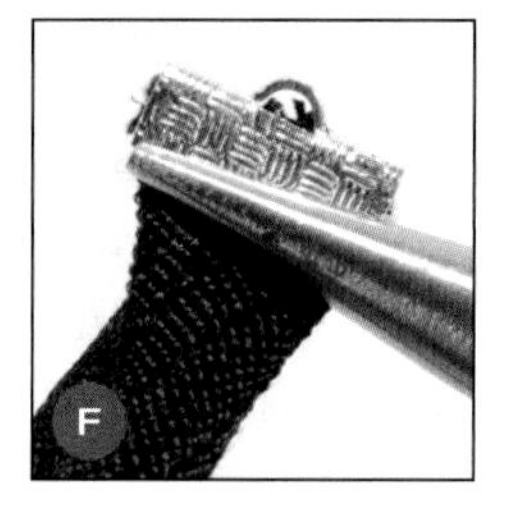

5 On one side, string a Bali silver tube over both pieces of silk cord and position it next to the jump ring. Repeat on the other side **E**.

6 Cut the silk cord to the desired length and glue the ends to prevent the silk from fraying. Place the ends in a C-crimp and use chainnose pliers to close the crimp **F**. Repeat on the other end.

7 Attach a jump ring to each C-crimp. Attach the extender chain to one end and the lobster claw clasp to the other end **G**.

Earrings

1 Cut a 2½-in. piece of bead chain. String a crimp tube on the end and flatten with chainnose pliers. String an 8 mm round cobalt/platino, a blown flat, and an 8 mm round aqua/platino **H**.

2 String the bead chain crimp end on the other end of the chain and crimp (basics) **I**. Attach the earring wire **J**.

3 Make a second earring.

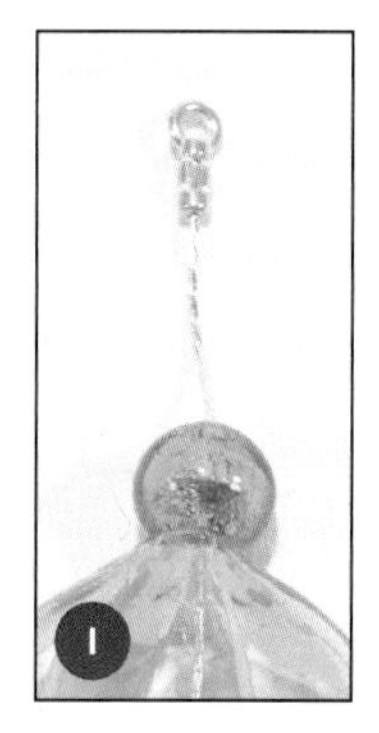

How to Spot Imitations

Genuine Venetian glass beads made from the Effetre cane produced in Murano have a quality like no others. The master bead artisans in Murano and Venice along with the secret glass recipes handed down for centuries have made spectacular Venetian glass beads for years. However, today when global access to inexpensive labor is almost effortless, it is imperative that one knows how to spot imitations. Even when visiting Murano and Venice, tourists will see copies of Venetian beads, vases, figurines, and pendants.

Black Fiorato beads—The imitation is on the left, and the genuine Venetian bead is on the right.

For years the easiest way to spot an imitation Venetian bead was to look for white powder in the bead hole. Since 1935, when the production technique of copper wire and nitric acid has been used, the holes of genuine Venetian glass beads have been clear—no white powder.

However, today some of the imitation beads are being "cleaned" to remove the white releasing powder from the bead hole. In this case, the hole will not contain thick white powder, but usually has a light white dust that can still be seen in the hole and occasionally on the outside of the bead as well. Also, it must be noted that the Venetian bead makers will use the old technique with releasing powder when beads have exposed silver or white gold so the nitric acid does not damage the exposed foil.

The genuine Venetian bead's foil is so thick it reflects the lights in the picture (left). The imitation bead (right) has barely any foil and you can see right through it.

Genuine Venetian glass beads have an evident glass quality and color difference that can be noticed by simply looking at the beads. The Effetre glass made in Murano has superb clarity and richer colors due to the quality standards maintained at the glass factories. In addition, the foil used for Venetian glass beads is thicker, creating a more luxurious appearance.

Many beads today are sold by hanks or by the strand. This is a very common practice for Chinese and Indian beads; however, it is not for the Venetian bead makers. Since the beads are individually made by hand, dipped in nitric acid, and then given a bath, the beads are packaged loose and in plastic bags. It is a very safe assumption that when the beads are temporarily strung they are not Venetian beads.

Visitors to Venice and Murano will find many beautiful beads and gift items that are genuine, but one must remain alert as there are many that are simply imitations. The thrill and excitement of seeing all the beautiful jewelry and shiny beads can be overwhelming, but it is imperative that we support the true artisans of Murano and Venice. Use caution and common sense, even when shopping in a reputable store, and look for the signs of the imitations: glass quality, residue in the bead holes, and of course price. As the saying goes, if it is too good to be true, then it probably is...

Venetian glass beads provide a rainbow of color choices; the range of glass colors and foils available translates to an almost unlimited color palate to work with. Whether used as focal or accent beads, Venetian beads flatter a wide range of jewelry-making elements including cord, chain, semi-precious stones, crystal, or other glass beads. Venetian beads also can be mixed with gold, sterling silver, copper, or even brass and look fantastic. Use them in a lush array, or sparingly to make a simple-but-elegant statement. Your design options are limited only by your imagination.

Jewels of Venice

foil lentil knotted necklace

Throughout Venice and Murano, beautiful jewelry is on display in gift shops. It's common for necklaces to feature the same shape bead throughout the entire piece, and it's also common for authentic Venetian glass jewelry to be knotted to keep the glass beads from rubbing against one another. One of my favorite designs is a knotted lentil bead necklace using a combination of three colors. This project teaches knotting the old-fashioned way—by hand.

Make matching earrings using the same knotting technique. Finish the end with a clamshell tip as in steps 7 and 8 of the necklace.

Supplies

- **33** 13 mm foil lentils in three colors
- **2** cards Griffin Silk Cord, size 8, in two accent colors
- **2** gold-filled clamshell tips
- gold-filled clasp
- G-S Hypo cement

tools

- chainnose pliers
- scissors or soft wire cutter
- fine point tweezers

1 Tie two silk cords together with a knot at the ends. String the clamshell tip to the knot **A**.

2 Place a drop of glue on the knot, trim the excess thread, and close the clamshell tip **B**.

3 Make an overhand knot (basics) around your hand and place the tweezers through the loop. Position the tip of the tweezers as close to the clamshell tip as possible **C**.

4 Remove your hand from the knot and gently pull the thread so the knot is tight on the tip of the tweezers. Make sure the knot is touching the clamshell tip and use the tweezers to push the knot tight against the tip **D**.

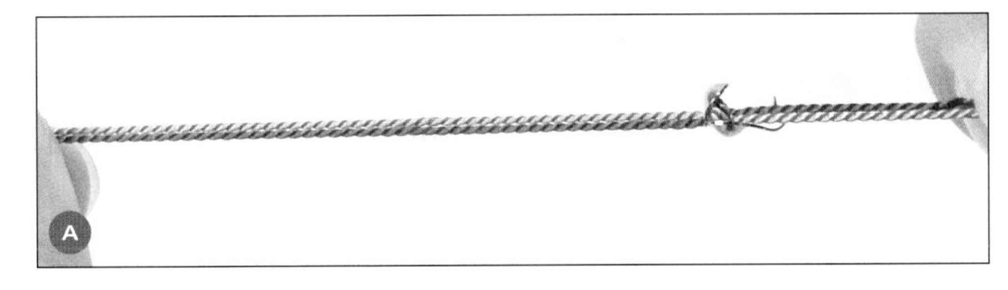

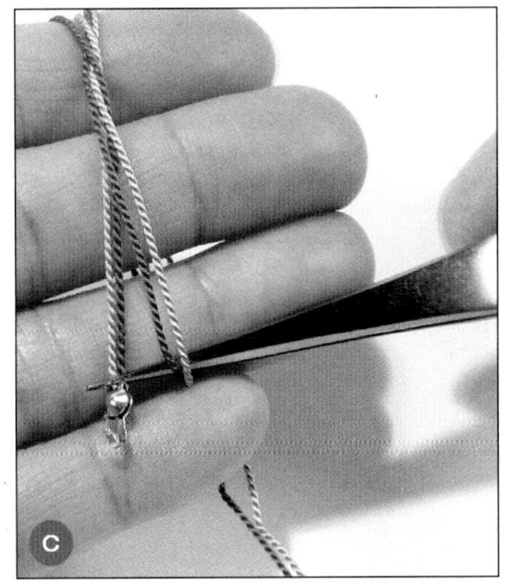

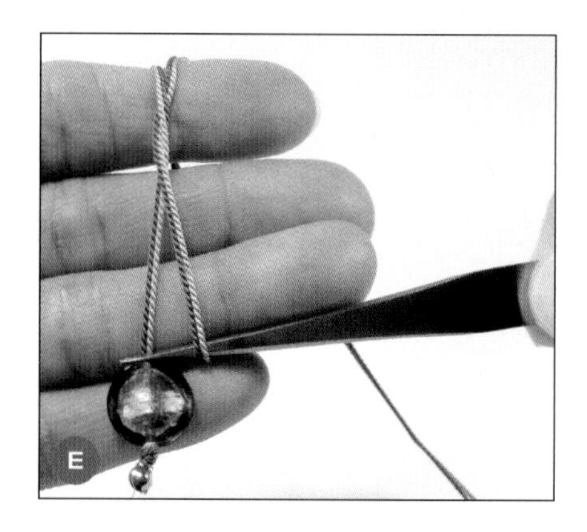

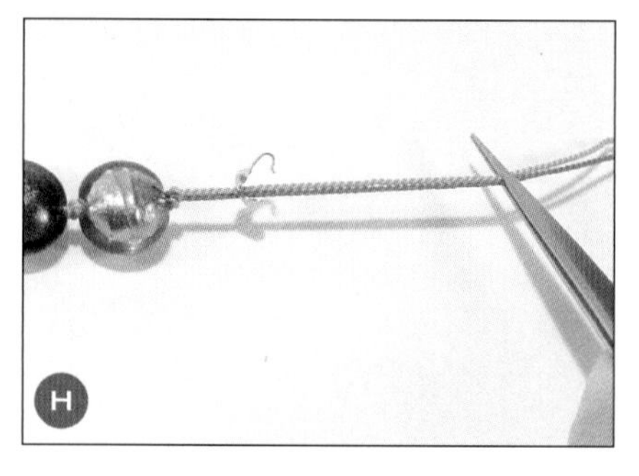

5 String a lentil bead. Tie an overhand knot and place the tip of the tweezers through the loop touching the top of the bead **E**. Remove your hand from the knot and gently pull the thread so the knot is tight on the tip of the tweezers. Make sure the knot is touching the clamshell tip and use the tweezers to push the knot tight against the tip **F**, **G**.

6 Repeat step 5, alternating bead colors until all the lentils have been knotted. Make a knot after the last bead.

7 String a clamshell tip with the loop toward the end of the cord so it is touching the last knot **H**.

8 Open the clamshell tip up so the tip of the tweezers fit inside the clamshell tip. Make an overhand knot, and manipulate the knot with the tweezers so it rests inside the clamshell tip **I**. Place a drop of glue on the knot, trim any excess thread, and close the clamshell tip.

9 Attach one half of the clasp to each clamshell tip **J**.

Stringing 22 mm disk and 20 x 20 mm square beads in this style of necklace is also quite popular and is seen in many stores in Venice.

Nero Bianco
crocheted necklace

While Venetian beads shine as focals, they also are perfect accent beads. Combining Venetian glass beads with a variety of other bead sizes, styles, and shapes is an economical design option. This necklace is truly a spectacular work of art that is easy enough for beginners yet yields stupendous results.

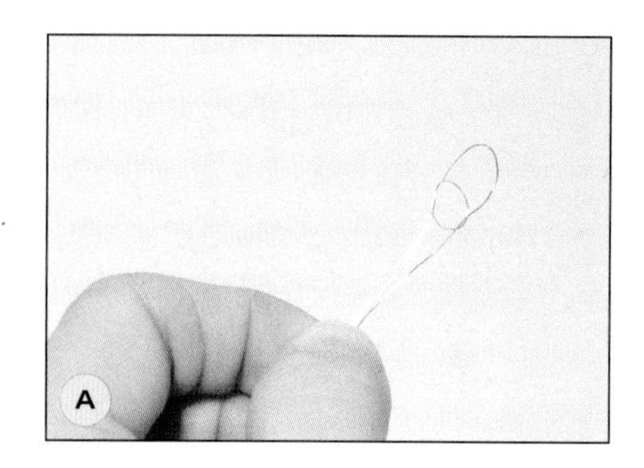

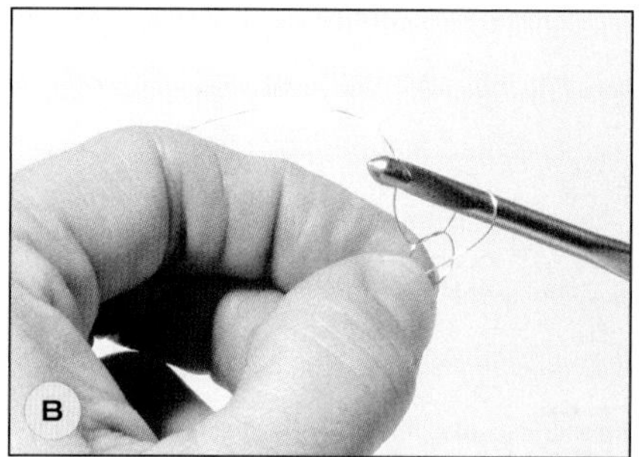

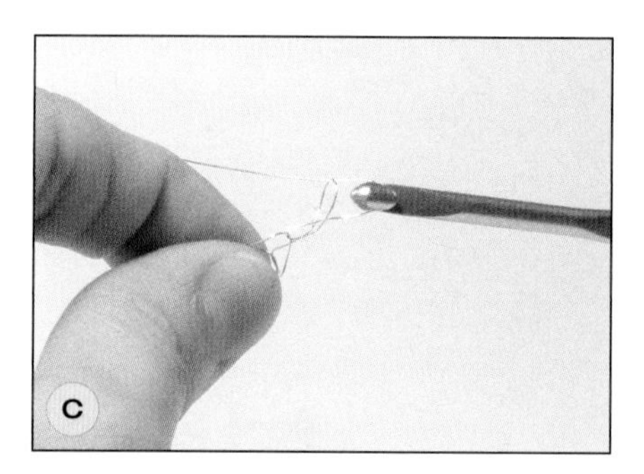

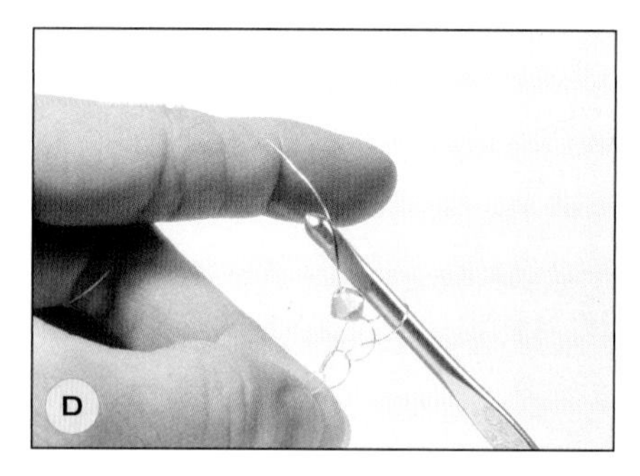

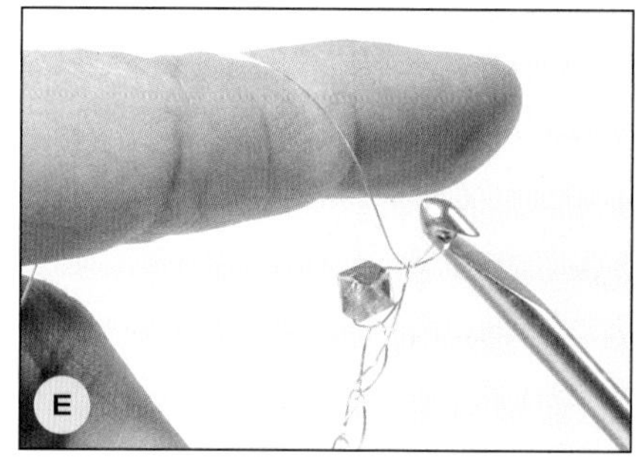

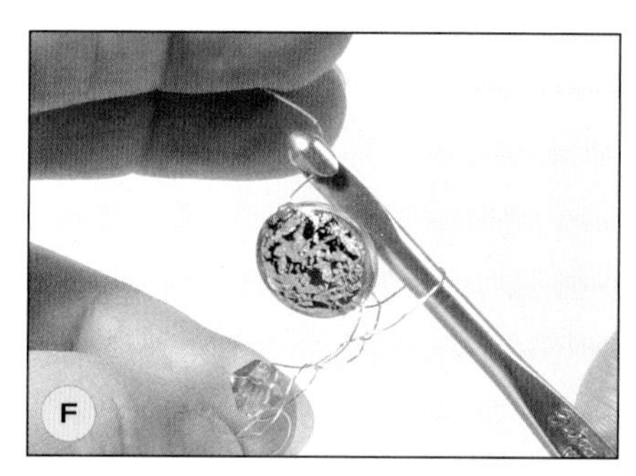

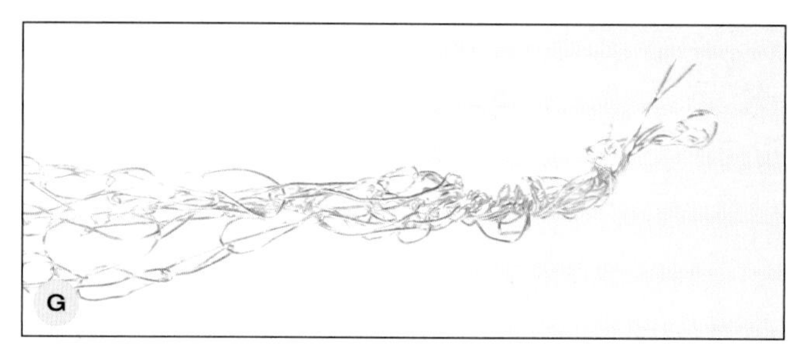

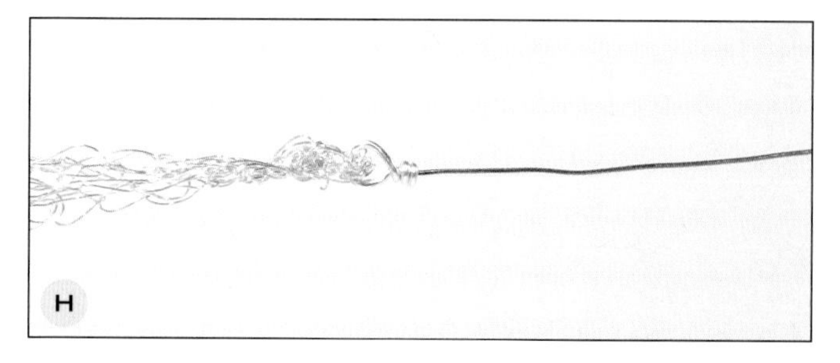

1 Keeping the 30-gauge wire on the spool, unroll about 3 ft. (do not cut the wire). Randomly string a mixture of 22–28 beads onto the wire.

Tip—Mix the beads in a bowl to help keep the selection process random. If there are a lot of smaller beads in the mix make sure to add a few more larger beads.

2 Make a slip knot by wrapping the wire around your finger and then pulling the wire through the loop **A**. Keep an approximately 3-in. tail.

3 Place the crochet hook through the center of the slip knot and grab the wire, pulling it through the loop to make the first crochet slip stitch **B**.

4 Repeat to make approximately five slip stitches **C**.

5 Slide the first bead down and make another slip stitch incorporating the bead **D**.

6 Continue to make two or three more crochet slip stitches **E** and repeat step 5 until it is the length desired, approximately 15 in. **F**. Cut the wire, leaving a 3-in. tail.

Tip—Vary the number of stitches between beads to help keep the placement random.

7 Repeat steps 1–6 until there are five completed strands of crocheted wire with beads. (Three strands also look nice.) Lay the strands flat next to each other and cut the ends even.

8 Twist the ends together **G**.

9 Cut a 4-in. length of 22-gauge wire and wire wrap a loop at one end (basics), inserting the twisted strands before completing the loop. Once the loop is wrapped, twist the wires again to secure them in the loop **H**.

10 String the wire through the cone, pulling the crocheted chain up as far as possible. String a 3 mm silver bead on the wire **I**.

11 Wire wrap a loop above the bead. Connect the loop and a clasp half with a jump ring **J**. Repeat on the other end of the necklace.

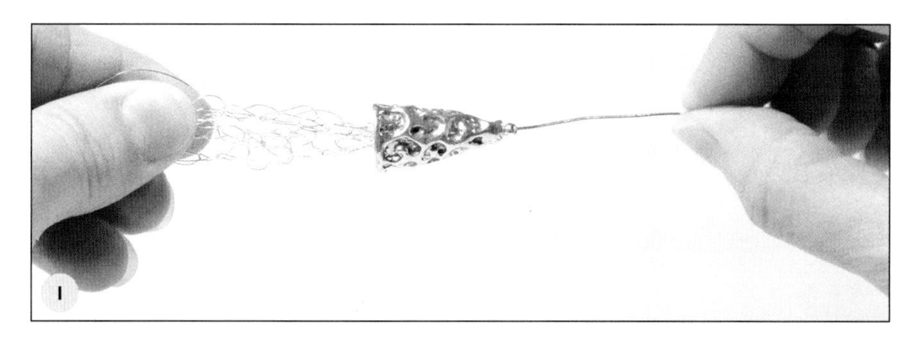

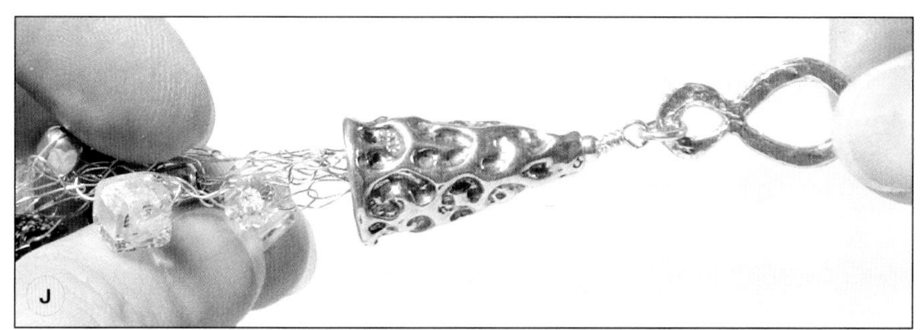

Supplies

- **110–140** beads of different shapes, sizes, and colors:
  - **10** 12 mm exposed gold rounds, black platino
  - **8** 12 mm cracked gold lentils, black platino
  - **15** 8 mm Swarovski crystal bicones, jet
  - **20** 6 mm x 6 mm foil cubes, crystal silver
  - **30** 6 mm Swarovski crystal bicones, comet argent
  - **22** 5 mm sterling silver square beads
  - **16** 5 mm Swarovski crystal margarita, crystal
  - **12** 5 mm Swarovski crystal margaritas, crystal/foiled
- **2** sterling silver 3 mm round beads
- **2** sterling silver cones
- **2** 6 mm 20-gauge sterling silver jump rings
- sterling silver hook-and-eye clasp
- ½ oz. 30-gauge sterling silver half-hard round wire on a spool
- 8 in. 22-gauge sterling silver half-hard round wire

tools

- chainnose pliers
- micro roundnose pliers
- crochet hook, size G
- flush soft wire cutter

Farfalla
Viking knit bracelet

Some Venetian glass beads are so awe inspiring they stand alone and make a perfect focal bead. One of my favorite focal shapes is the disk. A large Venetian glass disk makes a great pendant for a necklace, and a lentil or small disk creates an attractive focal bead for a bracelet.

Viking knit is a wire technique that dates to the 9th century and is still popular today. It seems fitting that an ancient weave frames an ancient bead. The technique is time consuming, but the finished product is most certainly worth the endeavor.

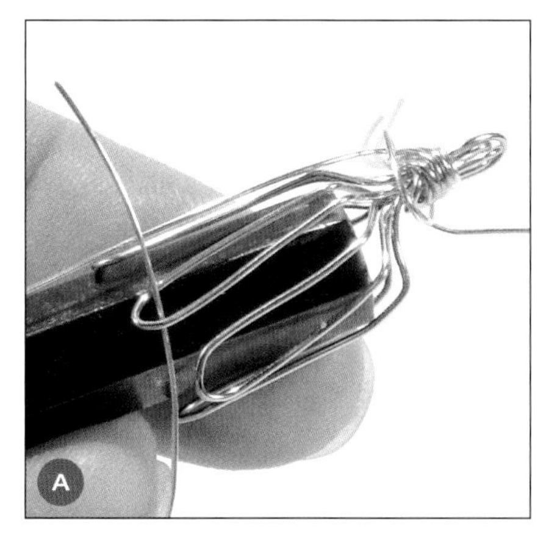

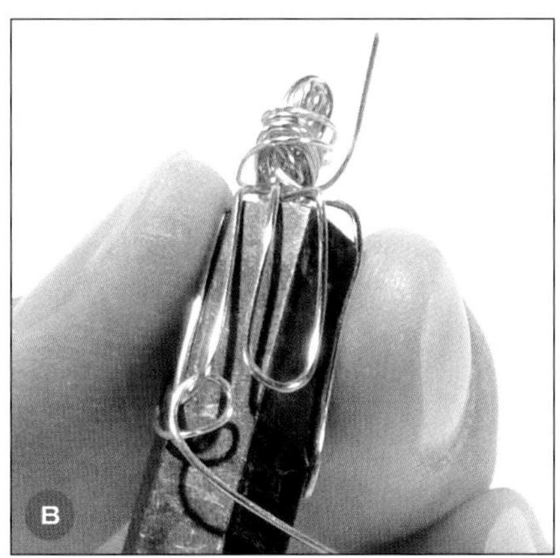

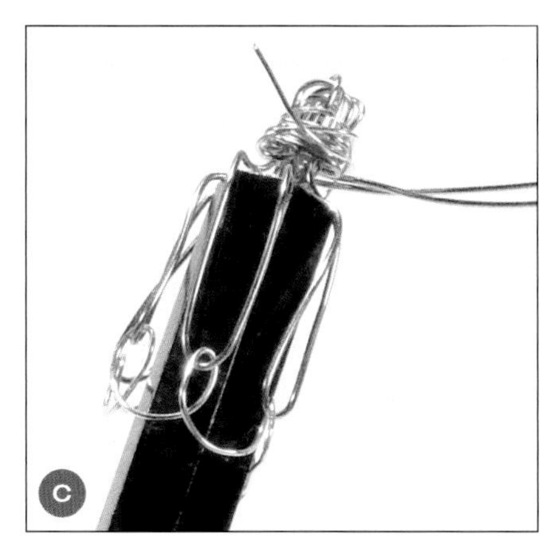

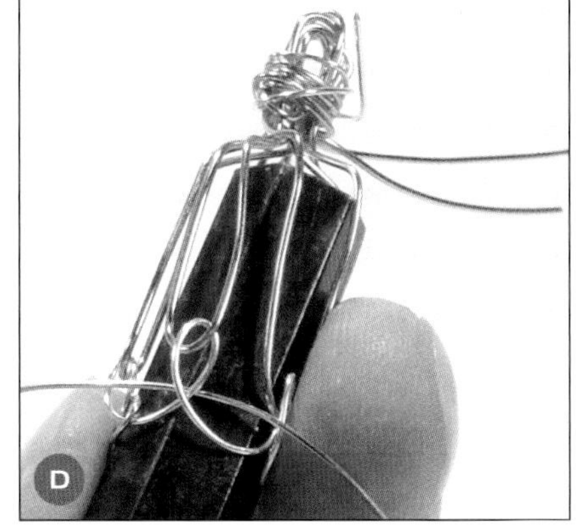

1 Cut 18 in. of 26-gauge wire. Begin Viking knit (basics) by inserting the wire down through one of the copper loops **A**.

2 Gently pull the wire down over the wire tail and up toward the next loop on the right, using your left thumb to hold the wire tail in place to make the first loop of silver wire **B**.

3 Continue clockwise, making the first row of single-stitch Viking knit by placing the silver wire and inserting it down through the next loop then over the wire swag until you have reached the beginning **C**.

Tip—Before beginning the second row, use a T-pin to make the teardrops and rows as straight as possible.

4 To begin the second row, insert the wire on the right side, behind the first row's X at the teardrop, bringing it out through the left side then over to the right **D**.

Supplies

- 22 mm Venetian disk bead
- **2** 8 mm Venetian foil round beads
- **2** sterling silver daisy spacers
- **4** bead caps (approximately 1⁄4-in. hole)
- sterling silver toggle clasp
- 25–30 ft. 26-gauge sterling silver round half-hard wire
- 2 ft. 28-gauge copper round wire (waste wire)
- 1 ft. 20-gauge sterling silver round half-hard wire

tools

- chainnose pliers
- micro roundnose pliers
- flush soft wire cutter
- 3⁄8-in. Allen wrench
- T-pins
- drawplate with at least a 7⁄32-in. opening
- ruler (1–11⁄4 -in. wide)
- tape

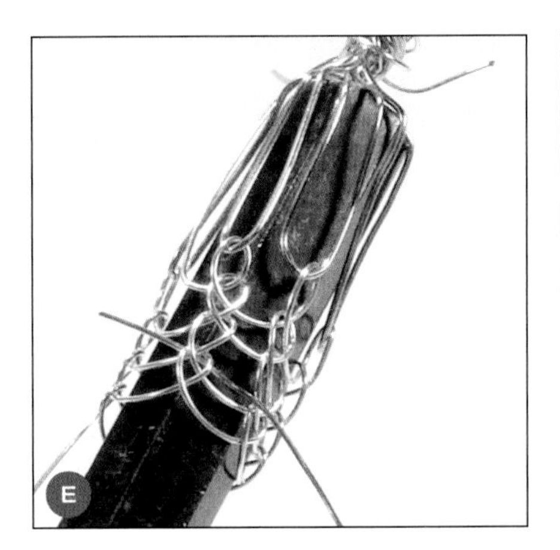

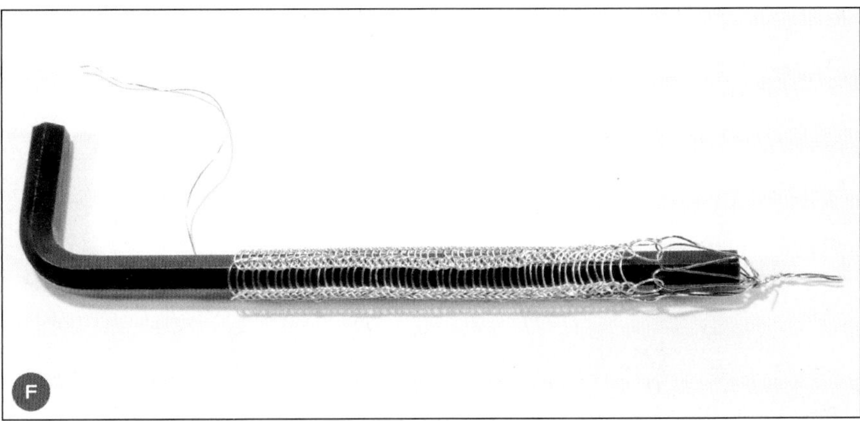

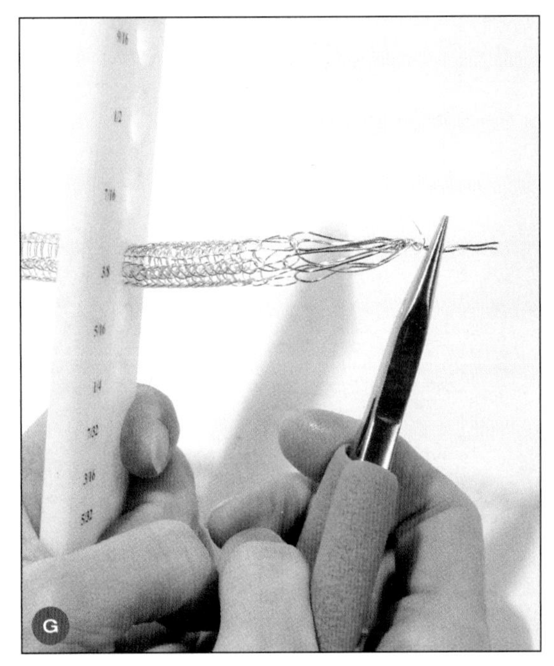

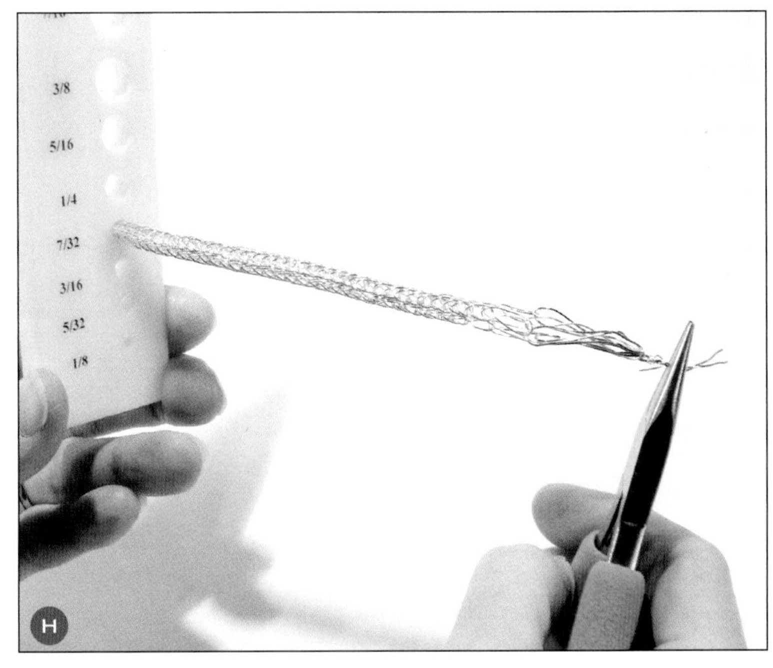

5 Repeat this around the allen wrench to make four complete rows of single-stitch Viking knit. Now begin double-stitch Viking knit to create a thicker finished weave. To begin the double stitch, count up two rows instead of one and insert the wire as previously done on the first two rows **E.**

6 Continue weaving until there is approximately 4–5 in. of Viking knit **F**.

7 Remove the Viking knit tube from the allen wrench. Begin to pull it through the largest hole of the draw plate. You may have to go through the hole more than once before continuing to the next size **G**.

8 Graduate down to smaller sizes in the draw plate until you are pleased with the thickness **H**.

Tip—Pulling the chain through the draw plate increases its length by 25%.

9 Cut the waste wire off. Cut two 2½-in. pieces **I**.

10 Cut 12 in. of 20-gauge sterling silver wire and wire wrap (basics) one end of the toggle in the loop. String the bead cap and one section of Viking knit on the wire **J**.

11 String a bead cap on the other end of the Viking knit segment and add the Venetian beads and daisy spacers **K**.

12 String the other section of Viking knit with bead caps on both ends. Wire wrap (basics) the end to the toggle **L**.

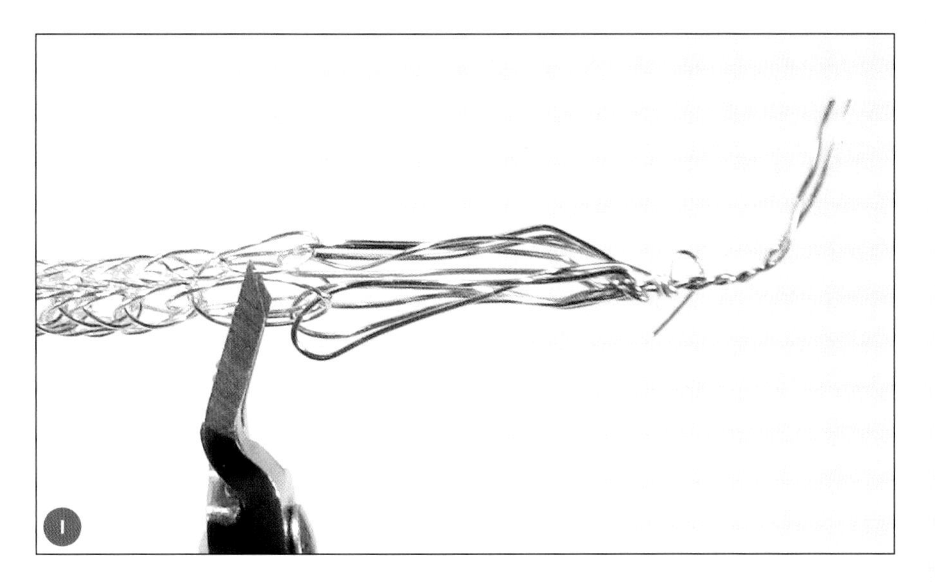

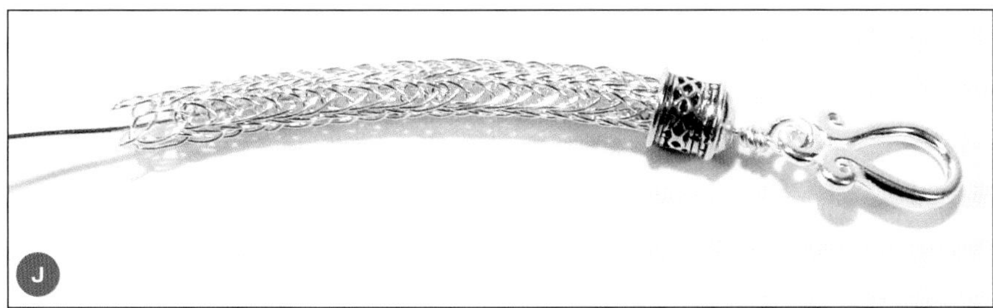

Designing with Venetian Beads on a Budget

While Venetian beads add glamour to any piece of jewelry, these magnificent beauties can be pricey and there are times when cost becomes a factor in design decisions. Obviously, the easiest way to reduce the cost when designing with Venetian beads is to use fewer beads. So the next question becomes, "How can one design a Venetian bead necklace on a budget?"

This project and the following two projects feature remarkable designs showcasing Venetian beads used in conjunction with other mediums that help reduce the cost of the finished piece, but do not sacrifice the splendor of the beads.

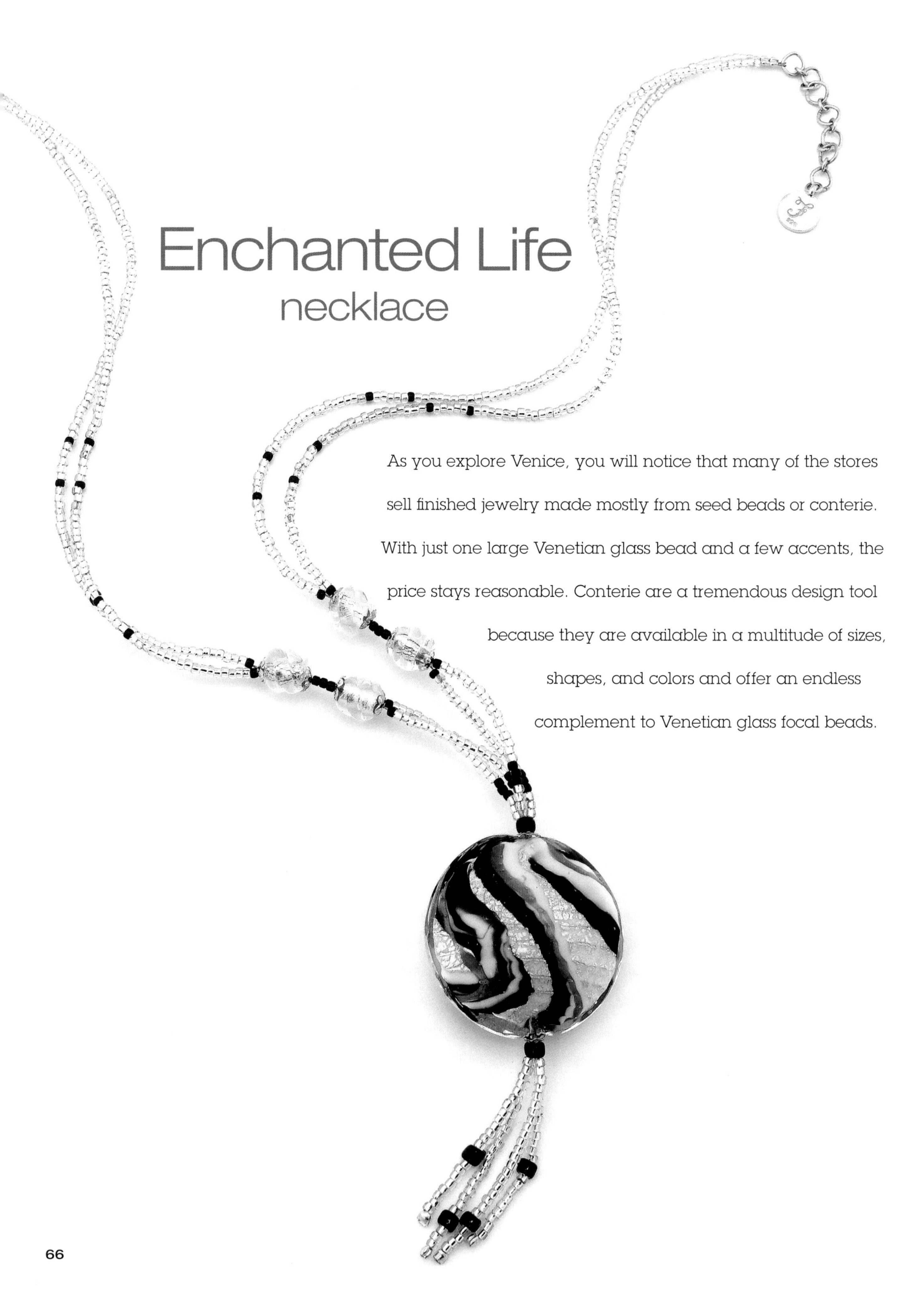

Enchanted Life
necklace

As you explore Venice, you will notice that many of the stores sell finished jewelry made mostly from seed beads or conterie. With just one large Venetian glass bead and a few accents, the price stays reasonable. Conterie are a tremendous design tool because they are available in a multitude of sizes, shapes, and colors and offer an endless complement to Venetian glass focal beads.

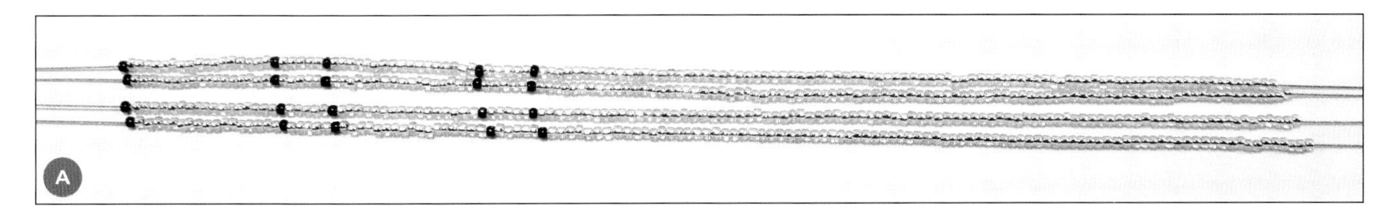

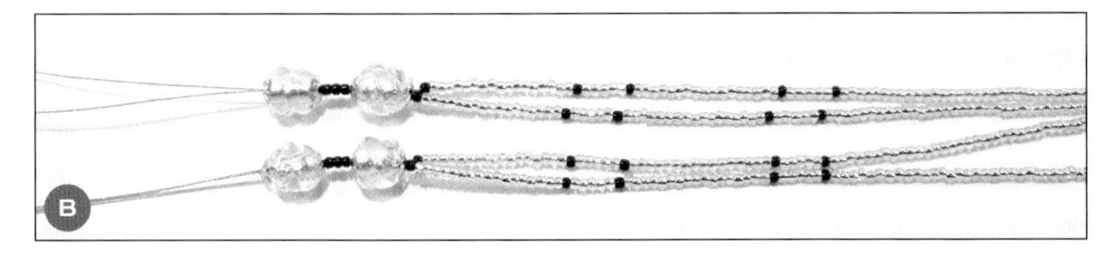

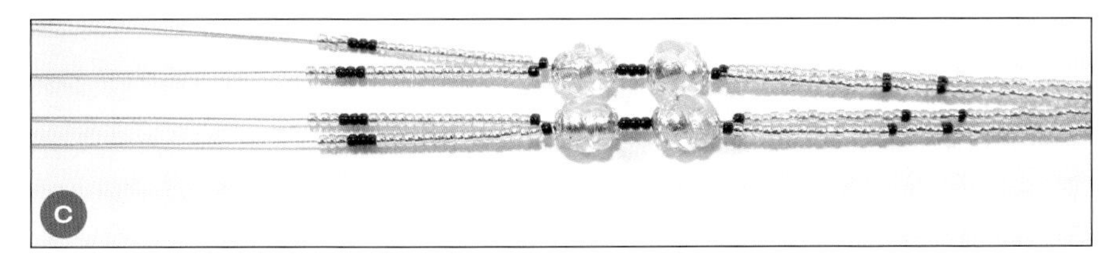

Supplies

- **4** 8 mm crystal oro melon accent foil beads
- large Venetian disk for focal
- 11º seed beads, silver lined gold
- 11º seed beads, black
- 6º seed beads, black
- lobster claw clasp
- 1½ in. of gold chain (for extender)
- **8** gold size 2 crimp beads
- .013 flexible beading wire, 49 strands

tools

- crimping pliers
- flush soft wire cutter

1 Determine the desired finished length of the necklace, add 6 in., and cut four pieces of beading wire to that length. Tape the ends to the work surface and string 11º seed beads in a pattern or randomly on the wires for about 8 in. **A**.

2 String two wires through a bead cap, melon, bead cap, three 11ºs, bead cap, melon, and bead cap. Repeat with other two wires **B**.

3 Separate the wires and string approximately 1½ in. of 11ºs on each wire **C**.

4 String all four wires through a 6º seed bead, bead cap, large Venetian disk, bead cap, and a 6º **D**.

5 Separate the wires and string 11ºs and a 6º on each to the desired length for the tassel **E**. Use one crimp bead per wire and crimp (basics) to finish. Cut excess wire.

6 Snug all the beads toward the large focal bead and remove the tape. Over both wires on one end, string two crimps and a lobster claw clasp. Go back through the crimp beads and crimp (basics). On the other end, string two crimps and the extender chain. Go back through the crimp beads and crimp. Trim the excess wire.

Vicenza Splendor
necklace

Stunning foil rounds float on the neck, like Venetian watercraft float on the canals. This minimal design maximizes value by using expensive beads sparingly. Vicenza is known for its precious metal jewelry; this necklace is named in its honor because it mixes yellow gold, sterling silver, and white gold foil Venetian glass beads with crystal rondelles.

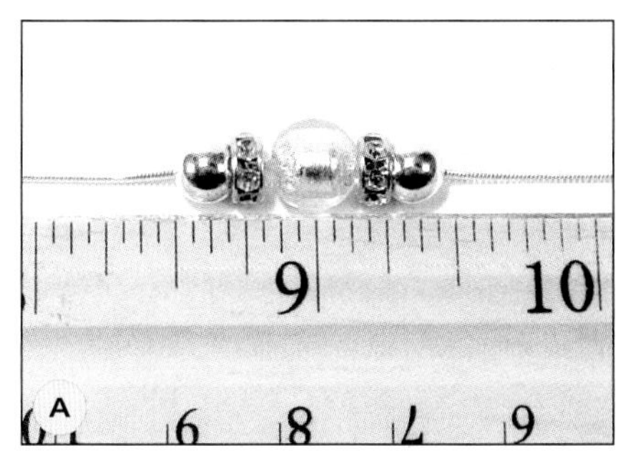

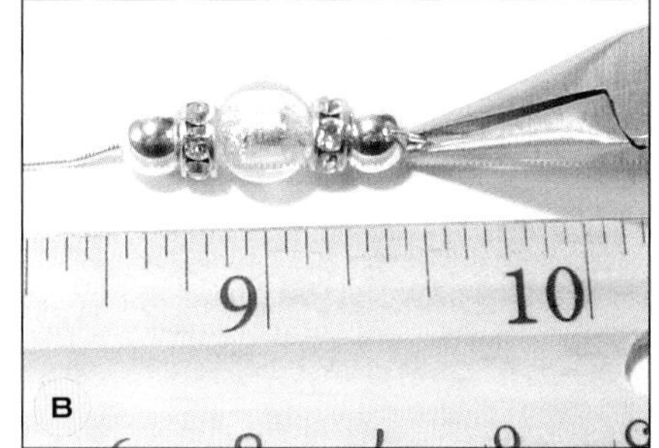

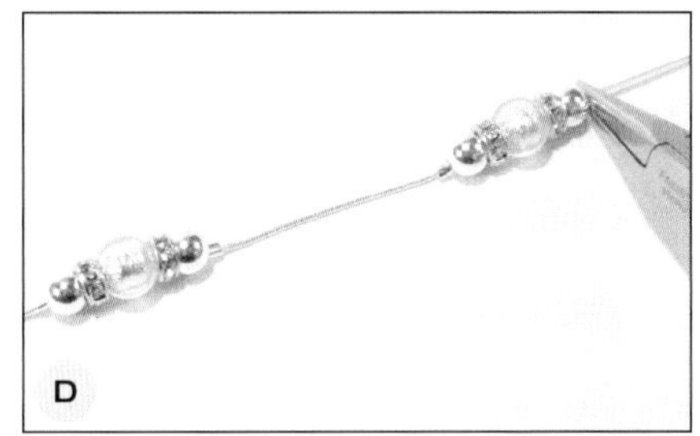

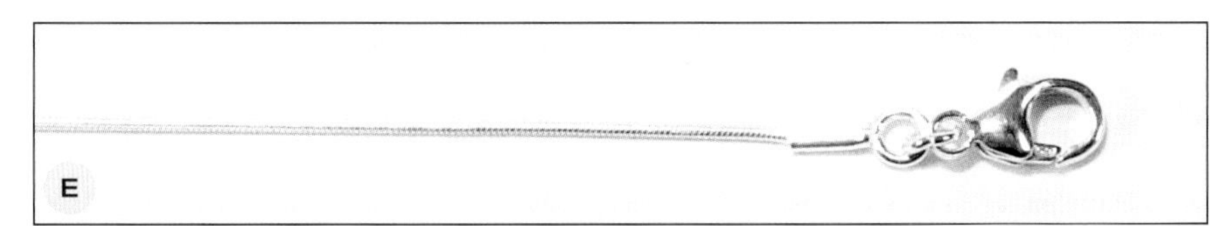

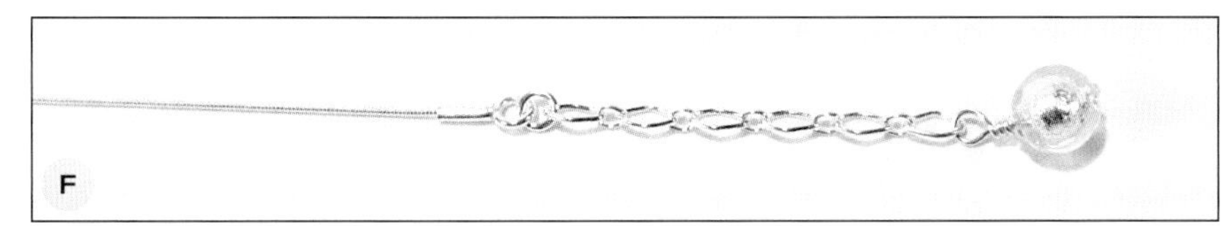

Supplies

- **6** 8 mm foil rounds, crystal/platino
- **10** 6 mm Swarovski crystal rondelles, gold
- **10** 5 mm round beads, sterling silver
- **2** crimp bead ends
- **10** size 1 crimp tubes
- **2** 4 mm jump rings
- 1 in. chain for extender
- lobster claw clasp
- 2-in. 22-gauge headpin
- 18 in. 1 mm sterling silver snake beading chain

tools

- chainnose pliers
- micro roundnose pliers
- flush soft wire cutter
- ruler

1 String a 5 mm round, 6 mm rondelle, 8 mm foil round, 6 mm rondelle, and 5 mm round. Find the center of the necklace at 9 in. and place the Venetian foil round at the 9 on the ruler **A**.

2 String a micro crimp tube on both ends of the bead section and gently squeeze the crimps to keep the beads from moving. Make sure the Venetian foil remains on the 9 as the center **B**.

3 On one end, string a crimp tube and position it 1½ in. from the crimp just made. Crimp the tube gently **C**.

4 String a 5 mm round, 6 mm rondelle, 8 mm foil round, 6 mm rondelle, 5 mm round, and a crimp tube. Crimp the tube gently **D**.

5 Repeat step 3 and 4 once on this end, and twice on the other end of the beads from step 1.

6 String the bead crimp end on a chain end and flatten with chainnose pliers to secure it (basics). Repeat on the other end.

7 Use a jump ring to attach the lobster claw clasp on one end and the extender chain on the other end **E, F**. Optional—string a Venetian foil round on a headpin and wire wrap onto the extender chain to make a dangle.

Tip—I prefer to start in the center and work to each side to help minimize spacing errors. Also, to help minimize costs, I do not make any floating bead sections behind the neck.

TRAVELS *to Venice*

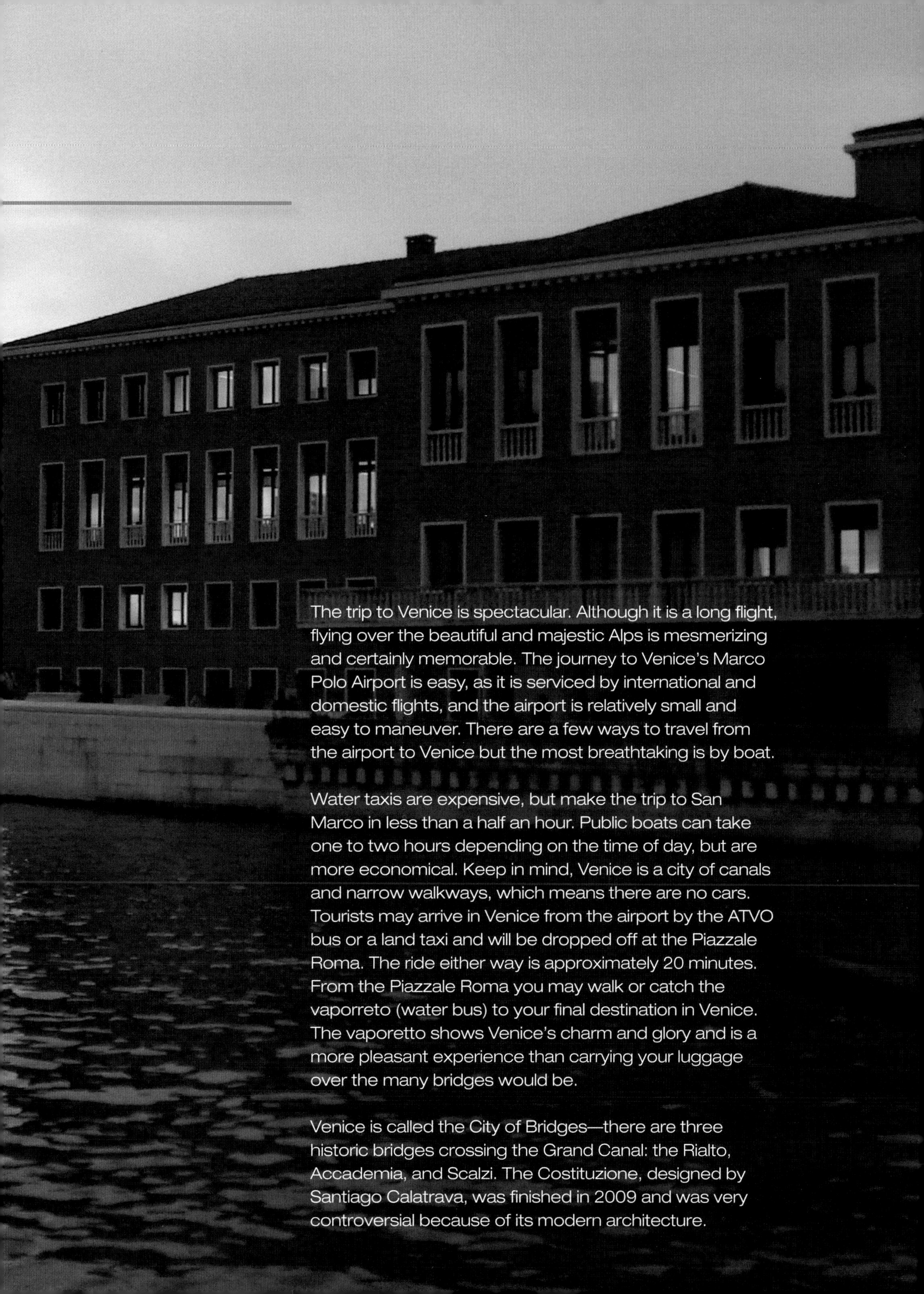

The trip to Venice is spectacular. Although it is a long flight, flying over the beautiful and majestic Alps is mesmerizing and certainly memorable. The journey to Venice's Marco Polo Airport is easy, as it is serviced by international and domestic flights, and the airport is relatively small and easy to maneuver. There are a few ways to travel from the airport to Venice but the most breathtaking is by boat.

Water taxis are expensive, but make the trip to San Marco in less than a half an hour. Public boats can take one to two hours depending on the time of day, but are more economical. Keep in mind, Venice is a city of canals and narrow walkways, which means there are no cars. Tourists may arrive in Venice from the airport by the ATVO bus or a land taxi and will be dropped off at the Piazzale Roma. The ride either way is approximately 20 minutes. From the Piazzale Roma you may walk or catch the vaporreto (water bus) to your final destination in Venice. The vaporetto shows Venice's charm and glory and is a more pleasant experience than carrying your luggage over the many bridges would be.

Venice is called the City of Bridges—there are three historic bridges crossing the Grand Canal: the Rialto, Accademia, and Scalzi. The Costituzione, designed by Santiago Calatrava, was finished in 2009 and was very controversial because of its modern architecture.

Piazza San Marco

You can experience Venice's charm in so many ways—ride a gondola on the Grand Canal, visit the sidewalk cafes, or shop at the Rialto Bridge to name a few. Piazza San Marco—St. Mark's Square—is a popular tourist destination. It was the heart of Venice's history housing the political, religious, and commercial functions of the day as well being a general meeting place. While sightseeing in the piazza, schedule time for Doge's Palace, the Clock Tower, the Bell Tower, and St. Mark's Basilica. Afterwards, enjoy a nice glass of wine at the Quadri or Florian's in the square. Of course, feeding the pigeons in the square has always been one of my favorite activities.

Doge's Palace, the Clock Tower, the Bell Tower, and St. Mark's Basilica can all be seen in this picture.

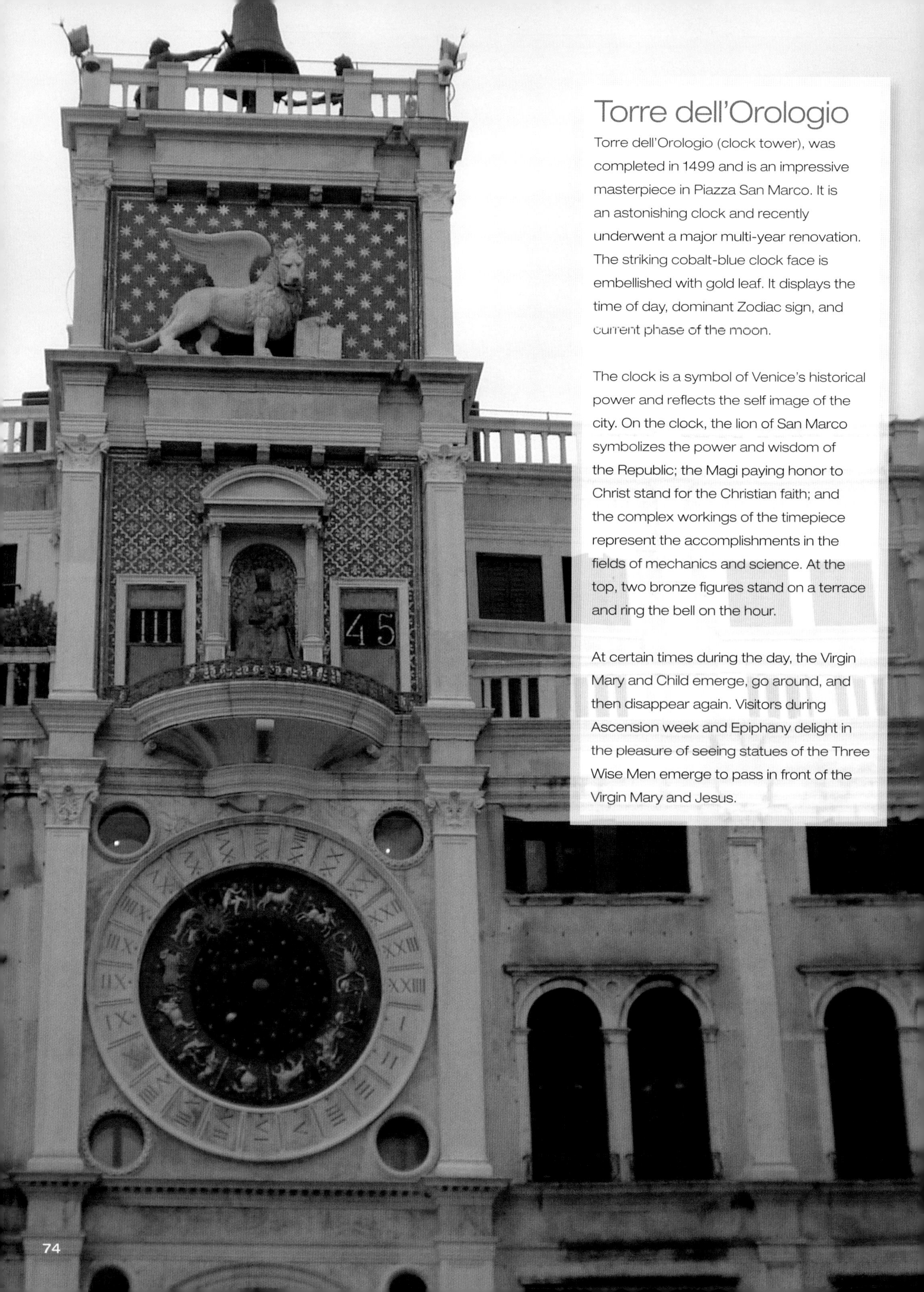

Torre dell'Orologio

Torre dell'Orologio (clock tower), was completed in 1499 and is an impressive masterpiece in Piazza San Marco. It is an astonishing clock and recently underwent a major multi-year renovation. The striking cobalt-blue clock face is embellished with gold leaf. It displays the time of day, dominant Zodiac sign, and current phase of the moon.

The clock is a symbol of Venice's historical power and reflects the self image of the city. On the clock, the lion of San Marco symbolizes the power and wisdom of the Republic; the Magi paying honor to Christ stand for the Christian faith; and the complex workings of the timepiece represent the accomplishments in the fields of mechanics and science. At the top, two bronze figures stand on a terrace and ring the bell on the hour.

At certain times during the day, the Virgin Mary and Child emerge, go around, and then disappear again. Visitors during Ascension week and Epiphany delight in the pleasure of seeing statues of the Three Wise Men emerge to pass in front of the Virgin Mary and Jesus.

Steampunk Torre dell'Orologio necklace

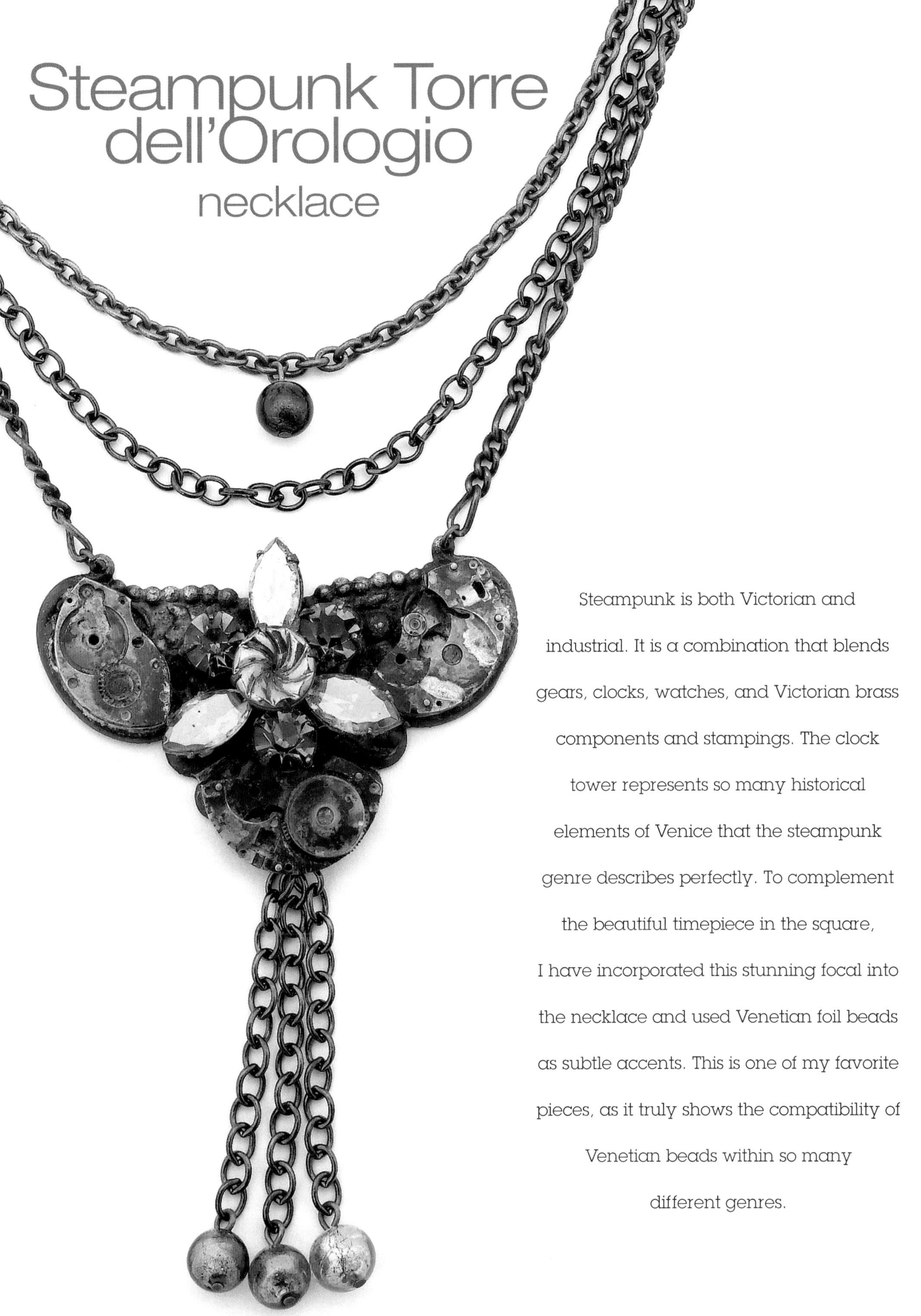

Steampunk is both Victorian and industrial. It is a combination that blends gears, clocks, watches, and Victorian brass components and stampings. The clock tower represents so many historical elements of Venice that the steampunk genre describes perfectly. To complement the beautiful timepiece in the square, I have incorporated this stunning focal into the necklace and used Venetian foil beads as subtle accents. This is one of my favorite pieces, as it truly shows the compatibility of Venetian beads within so many different genres.

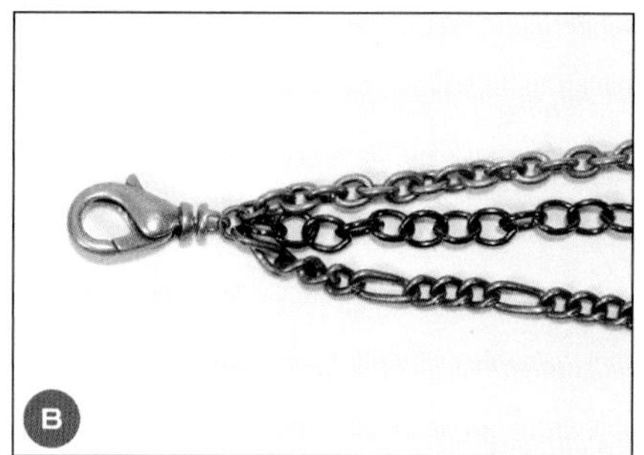

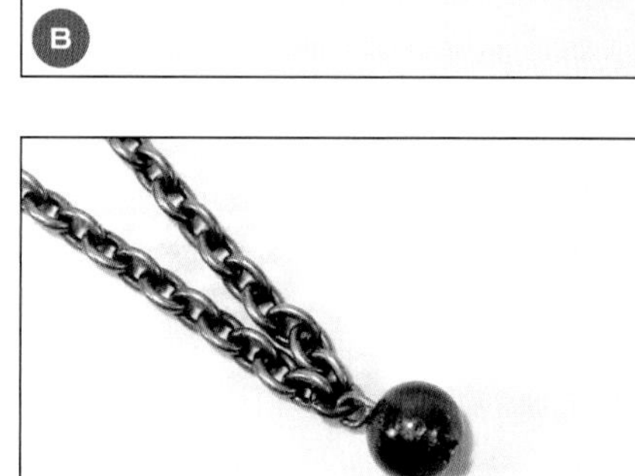

1 Cut two 10-in. pieces of brass figaro chain and use two 4 mm jump rings to connect it to the steampunk centerpiece (basics) **A**.

2 Connect the end of the figaro chain to an end of the gunmetal and brass cable chains with a 6 mm jump ring (basics). Before closing the jump ring, pick up the lobster claw clasp, figaro (outside), gunmetal cable (middle), and brass cable (inner) **B**.

3 Use a 6 mm jump ring to connect the remaining end links of chain (basics) **C**.

4 String an 8 mm foil round on a brass headpin and make a loop (basics). Attach it to the center link of the inner brass chain **D**.

5 Cut three 2-in. pieces of gunmetal chain. String a 8 mm foil round on a brass headpin and make a loop (basics). Repeat to make three dangles. Attach one dangle to each chain end. On the back of the steampunk centerpiece, attach two copper 4 mm jump rings together and then place the three chain pieces in the bottom jump ring to make the dangle **E**.

Supplies

- steampunk centerpiece
- **4** 8 mm round Venetian foil glass beads
- **2** 4 mm brass jump rings
- **6** mm brass jump ring
- **8** mm brass jump ring
- **4** 2-in. 22-gauge headpins, brass
- **2** 4 mm copper jump rings
- lobster claw clasp, brass
- 20 in. brass figaro chain
- 24 in. gunmetal cable chain
- 17 in. brass cable chain

tools

- **2** pairs of chainnose pliers
- micro roundnose pliers
- flush soft wire cutter

Campanile di San Marco

The Campanile di San Marco, or bell tower, is the most famous in Venice and stands 98 meters (322 feet) high. The tower was completed at the beginning of the 12th century and was used as a lighthouse for approaching boats. On July 14, 1902, the entire tower crumbled, permanently damaging four of the five bells. The bell tower was rebuilt and a ceremony to inaugurate the new tower was held on April 25, 1912. The bell tower offers an unbelievable panoramic view of the city and the most famous piazza below, perfect for capturing picturesque photos.

Casanova
necklace & earrings

As if it's a gift selected by the infamous Casanova himself, this necklace has all the beautiful purple shades Venetian glass offers as well as a lot of bling! Perfect for a night out or when you feel like some sparkle.

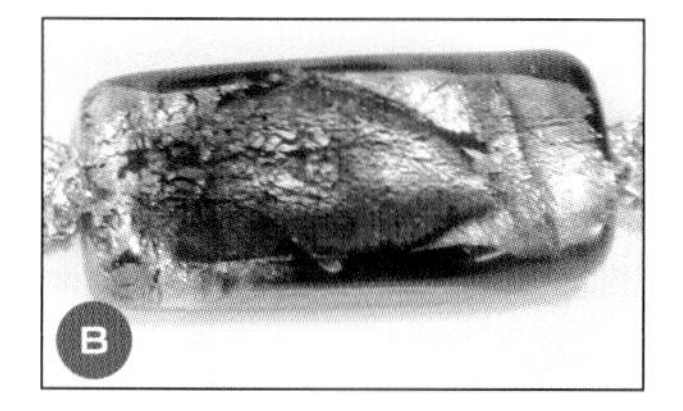

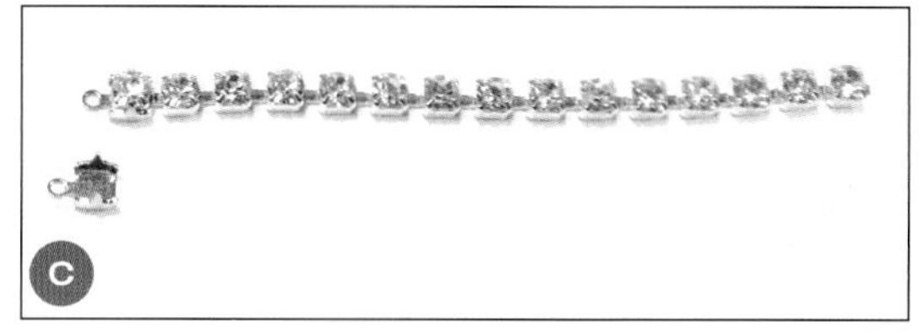

Necklace

1 String a rhinestone round, helix, 2 mm silver square, crystal silver twist, square, amethyst diagonal, square, helix, square, light amethyst twist, and a rhinestone round **A**.

2 String the butterfly rectangle **B**.

3 String the pattern from step 1. String a helix.

4 Set the rhinestone chain ends in the connectors **C** and gently bend the prongs to grip the rhinestones on the ends of all three pieces of chain.

Supplies

necklace

- butterfly rectangle, amethyst/purple/platino
- baby twists:
  - **2** crystal/silver
  - **2** light amethyst/platino
- **2** 15 mm Venetian diagonals, amethyst/platino
- **5** 8 mm helix-cut Swarovski crystals, purple velvet
- **4** 6 mm silver-plated rhinestone rounds
- **8** 2 mm sterling silver squares
- 4 mm silver-plated rhinestone chain cut into 13-in., 9-in., and 5-in. lengths
- **6** rhinestone connectors, silver
- **2** two-strand connectors, silver
- 8 mm sterling silver jump ring
- 6 mm sterling silver jump ring
- **4** 4 mm sterling silver jump rings
- sterling silver lobster claw clasp
- **4** size 2 silver crimp beads
- .018 flexible beading wire, 49 strands

earrings

- **2** 12 mm butterfly rounds, amethyst/purple/platino
- **4** bead caps
- 3-in. silver-plated rhinestone chain cut into two 1½-in. lengths
- **4** rhinestone connectors, silver
- **2** 2-in. 22-gauge headpins, sterling silver
- **2** 6 mm sterling silver ball-and-post earring findings

tools

- chainnose pliers
- micro roundnose pliers
- flush soft wire cutter
- crimping pliers

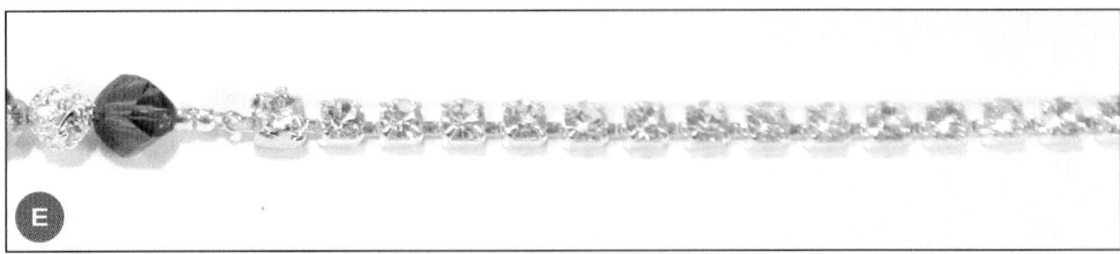

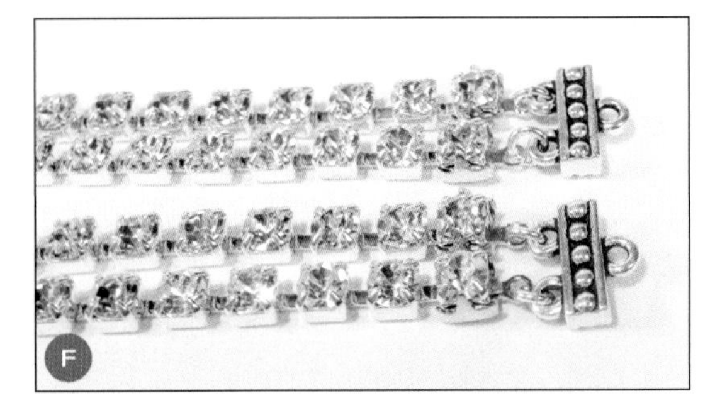

5 On the flexible beading wire, string two crimp beads and the rhinestone connector on one end of the 9-in. chain. Go back through the crimp beads. On the other end, string two crimp beads and the rhinestone connector on the 5-in. rhinestone chain. Go back through the crimp beads. Crimp all the crimp beads **D, E**.

6 Lay the necklace flat. Position the 9-in. chain next to the rhinestone and beaded strand. On each end, use 4 mm jump rings to attach a two-strand connector to the rhinestone ends (basics) **F**.

7 With the 6 mm jump ring, attach one end of a connector to the lobster claw clasp **G**. On the other end, attach the 8 mm jump ring.

Earrings

1 String a bead cap, the butterfly round, and a bead cap on a headpin. Make a basic loop (basics) **H**.

2 Attach the rhinestone connectors on each end of the 1½-in. chain lengths.

3 Attach a ball-and-post earring finding to a connector at one end of the rhinestone and attach the dangle from step 1 to the other **I**.

4 Make a second earring.

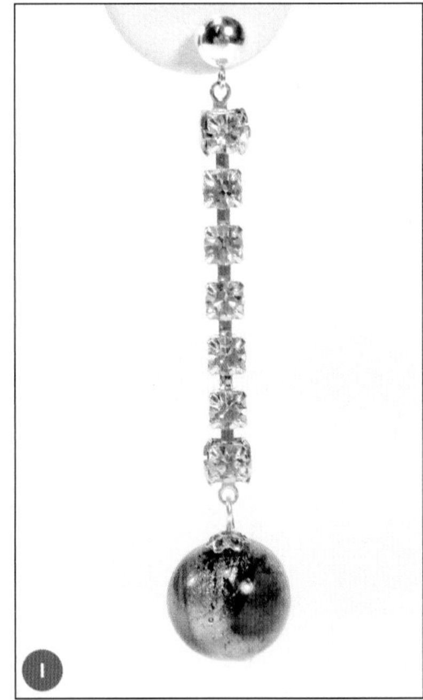

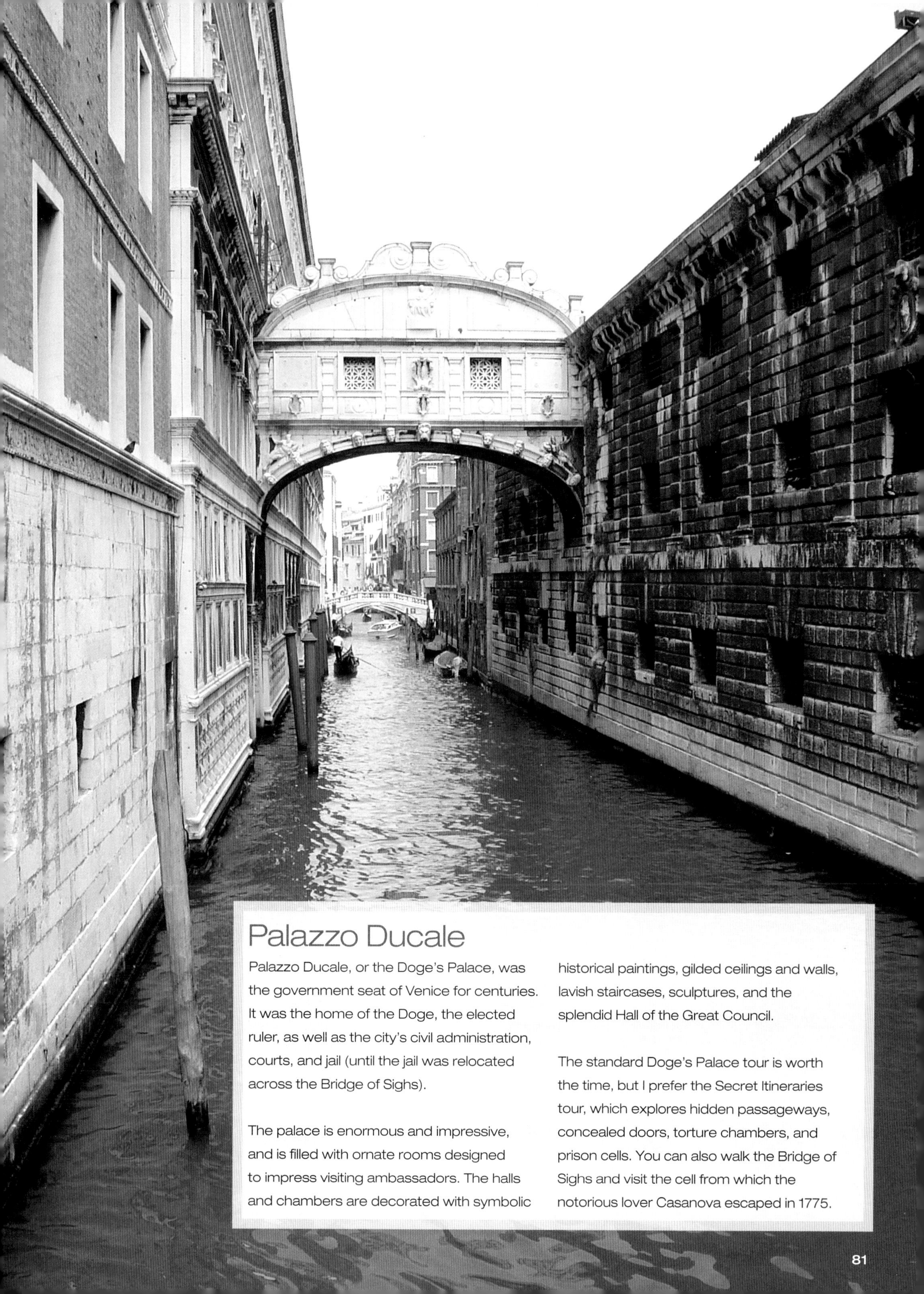

Palazzo Ducale

Palazzo Ducale, or the Doge's Palace, was the government seat of Venice for centuries. It was the home of the Doge, the elected ruler, as well as the city's civil administration, courts, and jail (until the jail was relocated across the Bridge of Sighs).

The palace is enormous and impressive, and is filled with ornate rooms designed to impress visiting ambassadors. The halls and chambers are decorated with symbolic historical paintings, gilded ceilings and walls, lavish staircases, sculptures, and the splendid Hall of the Great Council.

The standard Doge's Palace tour is worth the time, but I prefer the Secret Itineraries tour, which explores hidden passageways, concealed doors, torture chambers, and prison cells. You can also walk the Bridge of Sighs and visit the cell from which the notorious lover Casanova escaped in 1775.

Basillica di San Marco

St. Mark's Basilica, a breathtaking structure built in the 9th century to house the body of St. Mark, is located just off the Grand Canal. It was rebuilt from 1063 to 1094 in the Romanesque-Byzantine style and over time has been richly adorned with mosaics and decorations that bring together Byzantine, Gothic, and Renaissance art. It was the private chapel of the Doge's Palace; however, in 1807 it was declared the cathedral of Venice. The basilica's domes, walls, and ceilings are richly adorned with more than 40,000 square feet of gleaming golden mosaics dating to the 12th century.

Each time I visit Venice, I love exploring the San Marco area and finding something new. During a recent visit, my bead makers introduced me to a new bead they had developed. The captivating bead style reminded me of the San Marco area because it was innovative, but still had the charm and craftsmanship of traditional Venetian beads. The unique bead starts with a core of clear glass and then enamel is baked on to add the colorful design. These beads are delightful and add a splash of sparkle so I have nicknamed them "glitter beads."

Beautiful gold-leaf mosaic on the facade of the basilica depicting the procession of St. Mark.

LITHYMNS
UT VENETOS SEMPER SERVET AB HOST

San Marco
necklace & earrings

There are two historic cafes in San Marco that are the only survivors from the 18th century and although pricey, both are worthy destinations that capture Venice's charm. The Gran Caffe Ristorante Quadri and Caffe Florian sit on opposite sides of the square and have entertained noblemen, dignitaries, and the rich and the famous for centuries. In fact, Florian's was the favorite spot for Casanova while he searched for female company. Whether you stop by to sip a glass of wine, enjoy a cup of coffee, or relax and listen to the orchestra play, both cafes are true landmarks of Venice and great for people watching.

Gran Caffe Ristorante Quadri.

Caffe Florian.

Supplies

necklace

- 50 mm steampunk bullet shell
- **3** 28 mm Venetian oval beads, glitter topaz
- **2** 20 mm Venetian teardrop beads, glitter topaz
- 25 mm enameled oval connector
- 22 mm copper key
- 22 mm Italian coin
- 20 mm round steampunk connector
- **3** 15 mm enamel leaves, green and topaz (C-Koop)
- 15 mm steampunk gear, green (C-Koop)
- **6** 6 mm jump rings, copper
- **5** 2-in. eyepins
- lobster claw clasp, copper
- 8-in. copper cable chain, 10 mm open link
- 12-in. copper cable chain, 5 mm link
- 1-in. copper rectangular chain, 4 mm link

earrings

- **2** 20 mm Venetian teardrop beads, glitter topaz
- **2** 2-in. 22-gauge copper headpins
- **2** 10 mm copper cable chain links
- pair copper French hook earring wires

tools

- chainnose pliers
- micro roundnose pliers
- flush soft wire cutter

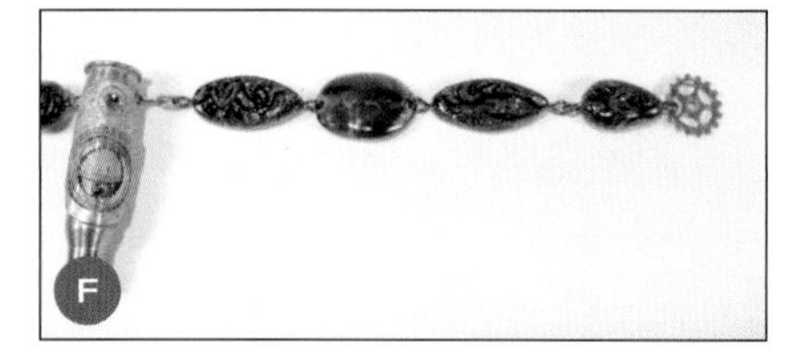

Necklace

1 String a bead on an eyepin and make a basic loop (basics) at the end. Repeat with all the oval and teardrop beads to make five links **A**.

2 Attach the lobster claw clasp to the end link of 10 mm chain with a jump ring, or by opening and closing the link **B**.

3 Attach the coin, leaves, and key with jump rings to the chain as desired **C**.

4 Connect an oval link and a teardrop link to each side of the steampunk link **D**.

5 Connect one end link of rectangular chain to the teardrop link from step 4. String the chain through the steampunk bullet, and connect the other end to an oval link **E**.

6 Connect a copper connector, an oval link, and a teardrop to the link from step 5. Connect the steampunk gear to the end link of the last teardrop bead **F**.

7 Fold the 5 mm copper chain in half and connect the two center links to the gear with a 6 mm jump ring **G**.

8 On the other end, connect a single link of 10 mm cable chain, the two 5 mm chain ends, and the 1-in. cable chain extender **H**.

Earrings

1 String a Venetian glitter teardrop on a headpin and make a basic loop (basics) **I**.

2 Use a link of 10 mm cable chain like a jump ring to connect the French hook and a teardrop **J**.

3 Make a second earring.

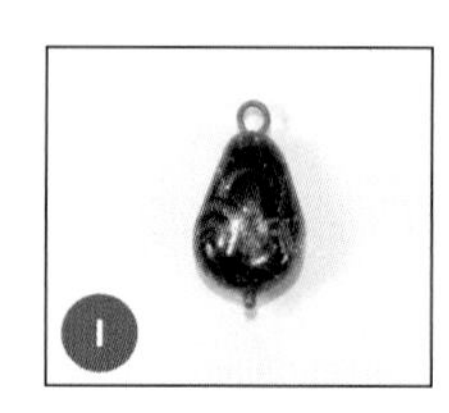

La Fenice Opera House

La Fenice theatre was the official opera house of the Venetian aristocrats and its elegant decor reflected a style of grandeur. Inaugurated in 1792, the theatre immediately took on a position of supreme prominence in Venice, reserving itself for the prestigious opera. Over the years, the stage has seen many prominent figures and continues to feature opera, dance, and music today.

La Fenice
necklace & earrings

The striking beauty and elegant splendor of the opera house is reflected in these filigrana Venetian beads. The subtle pink with avventurina hues swirl around the 24k yellow gold foil, creating a masterpiece suitable for front-row seats.

Necklace

1 Make the pendant: String a gold round, love knot, teardrop, love knot, and gold round on a 3-in. headpin. Wire wrap (basics) a loop **A**.

2 Center a 4 mm crystal, the teardrop pendant, and a 4 mm crystal on the beading wire.

3 On each end, string five liquid gold spacers. On each end, string a 4 mm crystal, love knot, nugget, love knot, 4 mm crystal, and seven liquid gold spacers **B**.

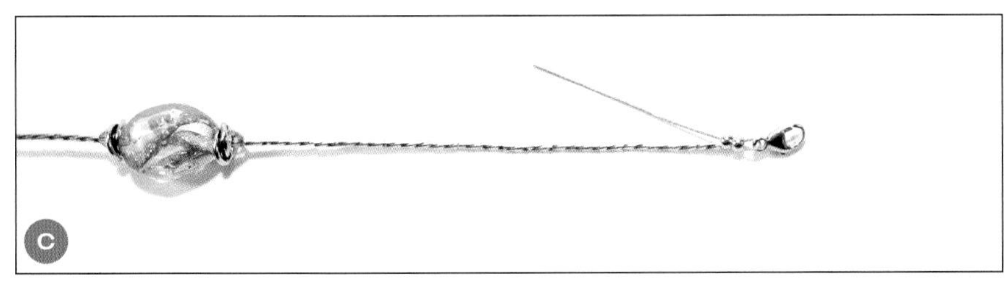

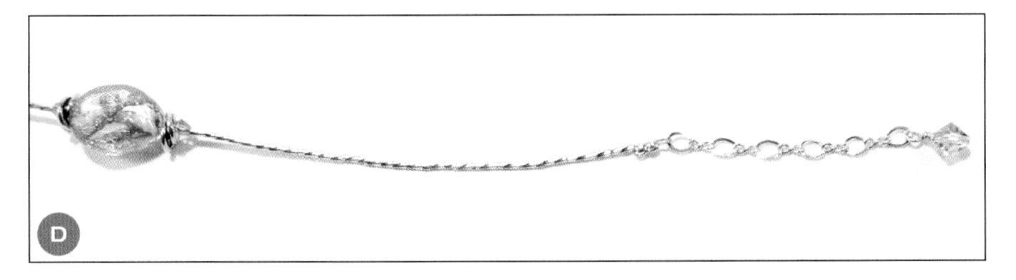

4 On each end, string a 4 mm crystal, love knot, 12 mm round, love knot, 4 mm crystal, and seven liquid gold spacers.

5 On each end string a 4 mm crystal, a love knot, a nugget, a love knot, a 4 mm crystal, and 19 liquid gold spacers.

6 On one end, string two crimp beads and a lobster claw clasp. Go back through the crimp beads, and crimp (basics) **C**.

7 On the other end, string two crimp beads and an extender chain. Go back through the crimp beads, and crimp (basics) **D**.

Optional: String a 6 mm crystal on a headpin and make a dangle by wire wrapping it to the chain.

Earrings

1 On a headpin, string a 4 mm gold-filled round, love knot, nugget, love knot, and 4 mm crystal.

2 Wire wrap a loop (basics) and connect to a French hook earring wire. Make a second earring.

Supplies

necklace

- Filigrana beads, rubino/oro
  - 30 x 20 mm teardrop
  - **4** 18 x 12 mm nuggets
  - **2** 12 mm rounds
- **14** 7 mm copper love knots
- 6 mm bicone crystal
- **14** 4 mm bicone crystals, vintage rose
- **2** 4 mm gold-filled rounds
- **76** 4 x 1 mm twisted liquid gold spacers
- **4** crimp beads
- 3-in. 22-gauge gold-filled headpin
- 2-in. 22-gauge gold-filled headpin
- lobster claw clasp, gold filled
- 1½-in. extender chain, gold filled
- .018 flexible beading wire, 49 strands

earrings

- **2** Filigrana nuggets, rubino/oro
- **4** 7 mm copper love knots
- **2** 4 mm gold-filled rounds
- **2** 4 mm bicone crystals, vintage rose
- **2** 2-in. 22-gauge gold-filled headpins
- pair gold-filled French hook earring wires

tools

- chainnose pliers
- micro roundnose pliers
- flush soft wire cutter
- crimping pliers

Lagoon

Murano

The Island of Murano is just north of Venice and is easily accessible by vaporetto (water taxi). The quick trip takes you past the cemetery island of San Michele on the way to Murano. Murano has many canals like Venice and also does not allow cars, but the atmosphere is much more serene than Venice. Rich in glass history, Murano today still has many showrooms of famous glassmakers, such as Lucio Bubacco, Davide Salvadore, and Pino Signoretto. It is of course a popular tourist destination, where you can visit the Museo del Vetro (glass museum). Small furnaces still exist where you can observe glassmakers in action. There are a few places to buy loose beads, but many of the beads you will find are basic foils. Some gift items, jewelry pieces, and beads are just imported copies. However don't let that deter your shopping spree—whether you are looking for a magnificent gilded chandelier, glassware, jewelry, or simply beads, Murano is the perfect place to purchase your own piece of history. Just be careful!

F.LLI MORETTI

Burano

Burano is a colorful island in the lagoon as famous for its lace as it is for its brightly colored houses. Legend has it that the colorful exteriors helped fishermen see their houses from the lagoon. As a small, tight-knit fishing community, the women made lace outside their houses while the fishermen were in the lagoon fishing. Soon the island became famous for its high-quality lace. Burano's Lace Museum, Museo del Merletto, lets visitors admire lace made locally over the centuries and occasionally hosts a lace making demonstration. Today women still sit

outside their houses and make lace. Burano is a 45-minute boat trip from Venice and while its personality is completely different, it has similar canals and bridges as well as Venetian glass jewelry in the shops. A perfect day trip, it is a nice place to walk the streets and enjoy lunch, soak up the local flavor, and photograph its main attraction—the colorful houses.

Torcello

Not far from Burano is the island of Torcello, the hub of early Venetian civilization. In the 5th century its population was more than 20,000; however, malaria set in and today it is a small community with less than 100 residents. There are few buildings on Torcello and the island is mostly marsh and fields, but as you walk along the lone canal to the town's piazza you will find two churches worth the excursion: Cattedrale di Santa Maria Assunta and Basilica Santa Fosca.

Built in the 7th century, Santa Maria is the main attraction and is one of the most impressive churches in the Venice area. One wall is completely covered in mosaics depicting the apotheosis of Christ and the last judgement. There is even a mosaic in the floor from the original church that is preserved and still viewable.

Santa Fosca is next door and is quite different. The church dates back to the 11th century and has an octagonal frame with three apses. You can admire a beautiful sculpture of Santa Fosca from the 15th century on the altar. The bell tower is a steep climb, but the view over the island and lagoon is worth the effort. In addition, the church's museum offers a small collection of archaeological finds and historical items from the cathedral and surrounding area.

Attila's Throne is a large stone seat said to be that of the 5th century king of the Huns.

Although there are not many restaurants on Torcello, it does have one of the most well-known restaurants in the area, Locanda Cipriani. Many famous guests have visited the Cipriani from Ernest Hemingway to Princess Diana. It is very pricey, but does have a lot of charm from years past.

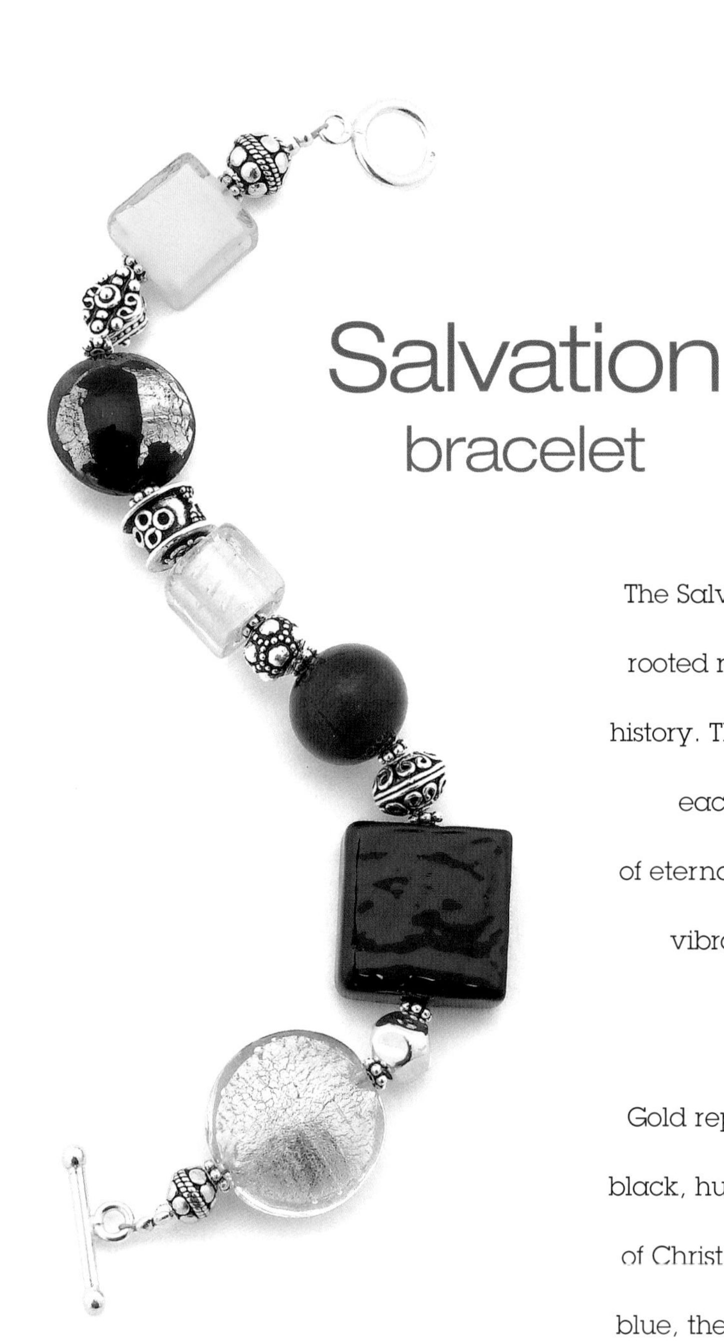

Salvation
bracelet

The Salvation bracelet is devoted to the deep-rooted religious faith represented in Venetian history. This bracelet tells the story of God's love; each bead color represents a symbol of eternal salvation. The rich gold foils and the vibrant colors help create this bracelet with a story and history.

Gold represents the golden streets of heaven; black, human sin and selfishness; red, the blood of Christ for our lives; white, God's forgiveness; blue, the Holy Spirit living in us; green, life and growth with God.

Basillica di San Marco

Interior detail of Basillica di San Marco (page 82).

Gilded mosaic on the façade of St. Mark's Basilica.

1 String an alternating pattern of Bali silver beads, spacers, and a Venetian bead in the following color order: gold, black, red, white, blue, and green **A**.

2 On each end, string two crimp beads and a clasp half. Check the fit, crimp the crimp beads (basics) and trim the excess wire **B**.

Supplies

There are many Venetian beads that can be used in this bracelet to represent the color themes. Below is the list of Venetian beads I used in the bracelet and the color represented is in parenthesis.

- 22 mm disc, crystal/oro (gold)
- 20 mm white core square, black (black)
- 17 mm abstract disc, bluino (blue)
- 14 mm white core square, lime (green)
- 14 mm foil round, red/oro (red)
- 10 mm foil cube, crystal/platino (white)
- **12** 4 mm Bali silver daisy spacers
- **7** 4–10 mm Bali silver beads, variety of shapes
- **4** crimp beads
- sterling silver toggle clasp
- .018 flexible beading wire, 49 strands

tools
- crimping pliers
- flush soft wire cutter

Mediterranean
necklace & earrings

As one of the most cheerful lagoon islands nestled near the Mediterranean Sea, Burano and its colorful personality can be reflected by many of the color combinations captured in Venetian foil beads. Whether it is a deep or bright sky blue, an intense purple, or even a brilliant sunset pink, there are so many beautiful colors to work with. Designing with bicolor beads, I chose aqua platino to represent the brilliant blue of the Mediterranean Sea and accented with lime platino to symbolize colorful Burano.

Supplies

necklace

- 22 mm Venetian bicolor disc, aqua/lime/platino
- 15 mm Venetian foil twist, lime/platino
- **2** 10 mm Venetian foil rounds, lime/platino
- 10 mm Venetian foil round, aqua/platino
- 10 mm round crystal, capri blue
- **2** 6 mm bicone crystals, peridot 2AB
- **2** 3 mm sterling silver round beads
- **10** 2 mm sterling silver round beads
- 3-in. 22-gauge sterling silver headpin
- **12** 6 mm sterling silver jump rings
- sterling silver toggle clasp
- 15-in. 22-gauge sterling silver round half-hard wire
- 18-in. hammered sterling silver chain (10 and 15 mm round links)
- 3-in. hammered sterling silver accent chain (10 mm oval links)

earrings

- **2** 15 mm Venetian foil twists, lime/platino
- **2** 2-link segments of large-and-small chain
- **4** 2 mm sterling silver round beads
- **2** 2-in. 22-gauge sterling silver headpins
- **2** 4 mm sterling silver jump rings
- pair sterling silver French hook earring wires

tools

- chainnose pliers
- micro roundnose pliers
- flush soft wire cutter

Necklace

1 Cut four 3-in. pieces of wire. On one end of each wire make a loop (basics). String:

- a 2 mm round, a 10 mm crystal round, and a 2 mm round
- a 2 mm round, a 10 mm lime/platino round, and a 2 mm round
- a 6 mm bicone, a 2 mm round, a 10 mm aqua/platino round, a 2 mm round, and a 6 mm bicone
- a 2 mm round, a twist, and a 2 mm round

Make a loop at the end of each beaded wire **A**.

2 Cut the large chain to three 3-in. lengths and one 11½-in. length. (Lengths may vary depending on the chain style.) Use jump rings to connect segments in the following order: the bar toggle, a 3-in. length, the twist link, a 3-in. length, and the round/bicone link **B**.

3 Use jump rings to connect the 11½-in. segment to the round/bicone link, and to connect the lime round link and a 3-in. length **C**.

4 Use jump rings to connect the crystal round link and the small chain **D**.

5 Connect the loop half of the clasp to the end of the small chain. On the other side of the toggle, use a jump ring to connect a single large link of chain. Connect a jump ring to the link **E**.

6 String a 3 mm round, the bicolor disc, and a 3 mm round on a headpin. Wire wrap (basics) a loop. On a 3-in. piece of wire, make a loop at one end. String a 2 mm round, a 10 mm round lime/platino, and a 2 mm round. Make a loop above the beads **F**.

7 Use jump rings to connect the disc to the 10 mm round link. Connect the link to the jump ring attached to the toggle **G**.

Earrings

1 String a 2 mm round and a twist on a headpin. Wire wrap a loop above the beads.

2 Connect the link from step 1 to the large chain link with a jump ring.

3 Connect the small chain link to an earring wire.

4 Make a second earring.

BASICS

Basic Beading Techniques

loops, crimp beads, crimp tubes, chain crimp, crimp covers

Basic Loop

1 Bend the headpin above the bead in a 90-degree angle. Trim the wire to 10 mm. Grip the wire at the end with micro roundnose pliers **A**.

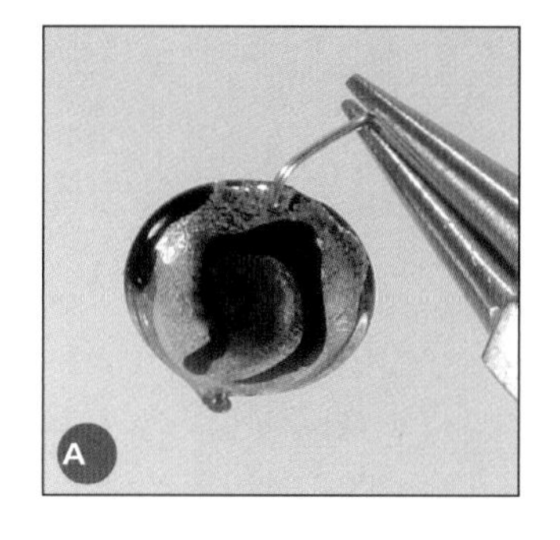

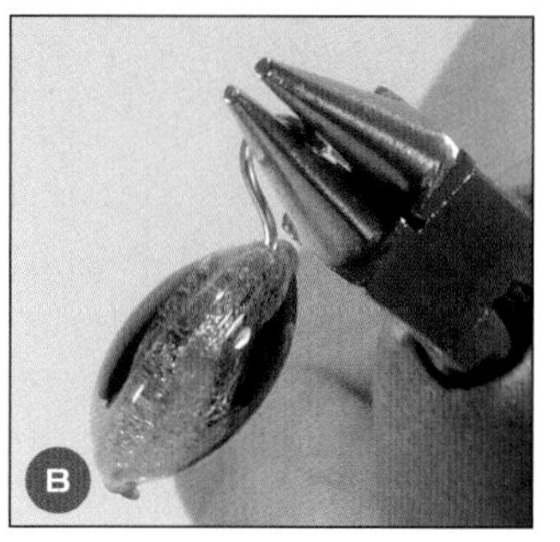

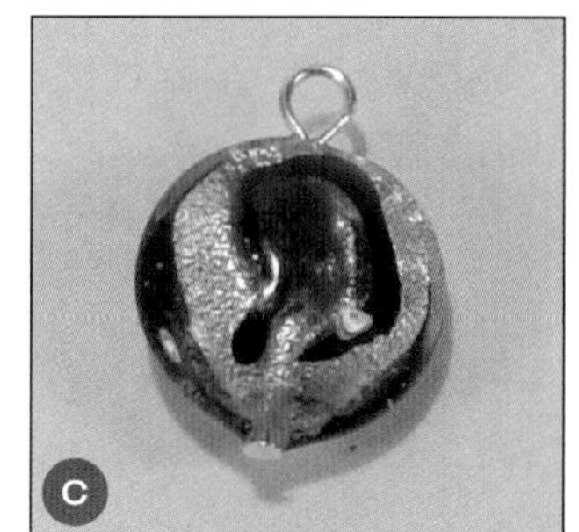

2 Roll the pliers to make a loop **B**.

3 The finished loop **C**.

Wire Wrapping

1 Hold the wire above the bead with chainnose pliers. Bend the wire at a 90-degree angle away from you **A**.

2 Position the micro roundnose pliers in the bend **B**.

3 Bring the wire up and over the top jaw of the pliers so it is parallel to the wire stem from step 1. Reposition the pliers, and continue to shape the wire around the bottom of the pliers. At this point, the loop can be linked to another component.

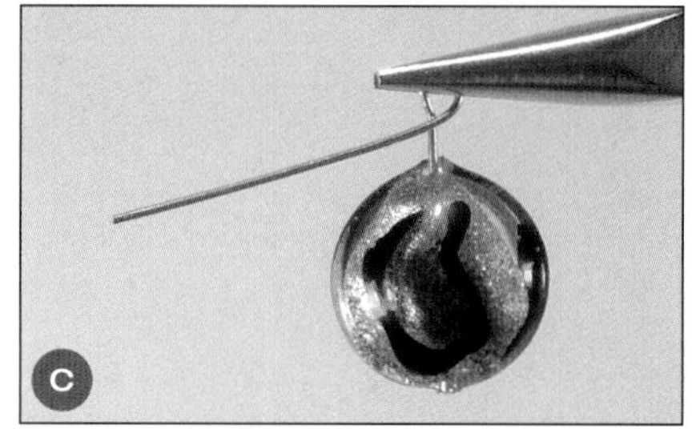

4 Grasp the loop with chainnose pliers **C**.

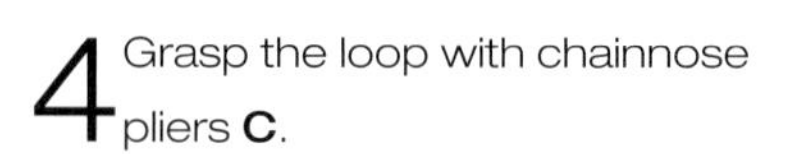

5 Grip the end of the wire with a second pair of pliers and wrap the wire three times around to complete the loop. Trim the excess wire **D**.

Crimp Beads

1 String two crimp beads and a clasp half on the beading wire. Go back through the crimp beads and tighten the wire.

2 Position the crimp bead closest to the clasp in the back notch of the crimping pliers (closest to the handles). Squeeze firmly, creating a groove in the bead. Repeat with the second crimp bead.

3 Check to see that the crimps are secure and trim the excess wire.

4 Repeat on the other end with the remaining clasp half.

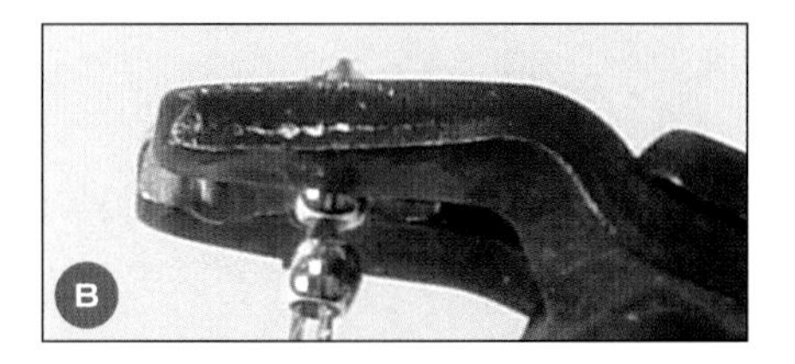

Crimp Tubes

1 Position the crimp tube in the notch closest to the crimping pliers' handle.

2 Separate the wires and firmly squeeze the crimp tube.

3 Move the crimp tube into the notch at the pliers' tip and hold as shown. Squeeze the crimp tube, folding it in half at the indentation.

4 Test that the folded crimp is secure.

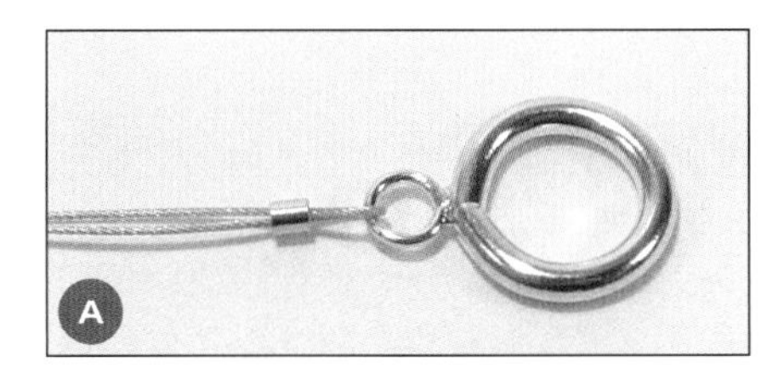

B

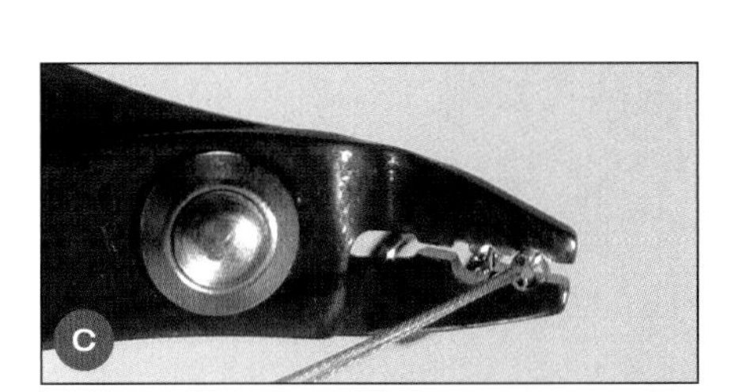

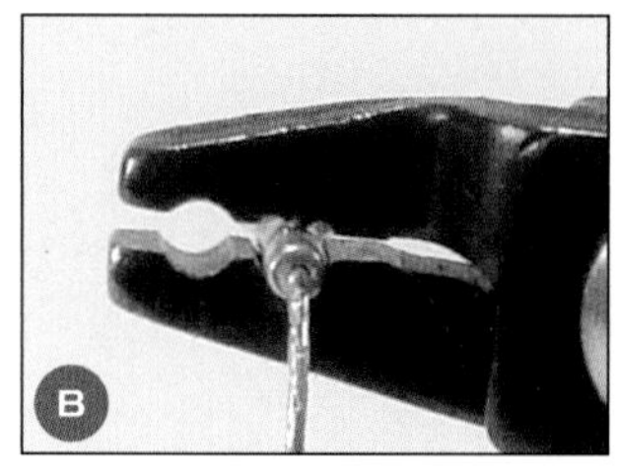

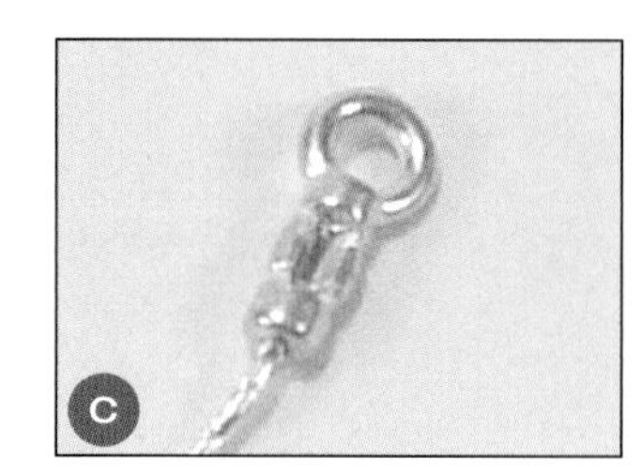

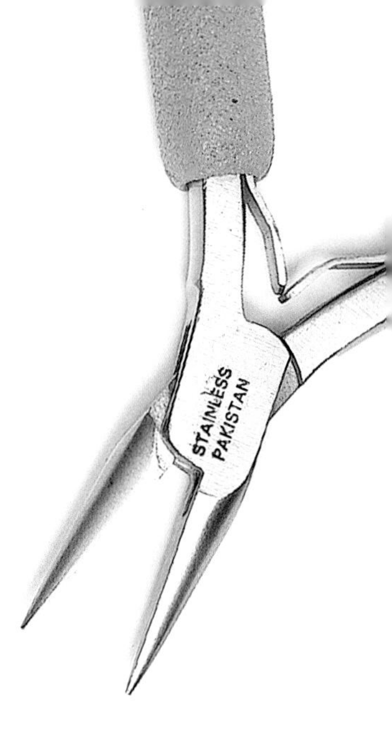

Bead Chain Crimp

1 String the bead chain end on the chain and make sure that there is no chain in the loop **A**.

2 Place the bead chain end in crimping pliers in the notch closest to your hand and squeeze to crimp **B**.

3 You should have an indentation in the middle of your bead chain end and the end should not move **C**.

Opening Jump Rings & Loops

1 With your right hand, place the chainnose pliers over half of the jump ring with the opening at the top **A**.

2 With your left hand, grip the jump ring with a second pair of chainnose pliers in the middle of the opposite side **B**.

3 With your left hand, move the chainnose pliers towards you to open the jump ring **C**.

4 Reverse step 3 to close the jump ring **D**.

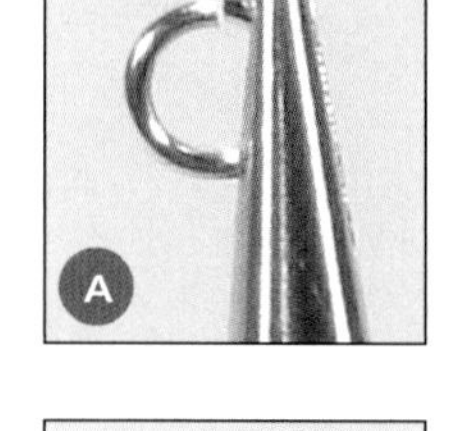

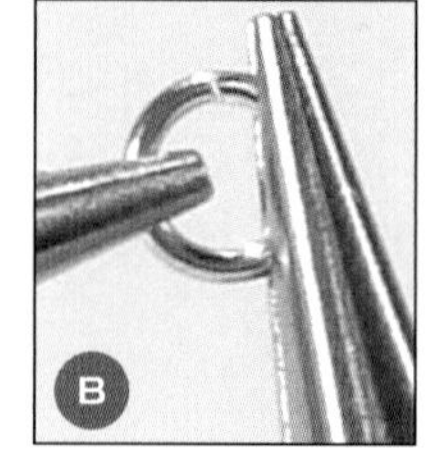

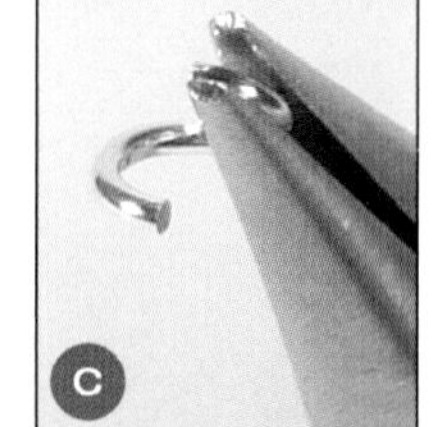

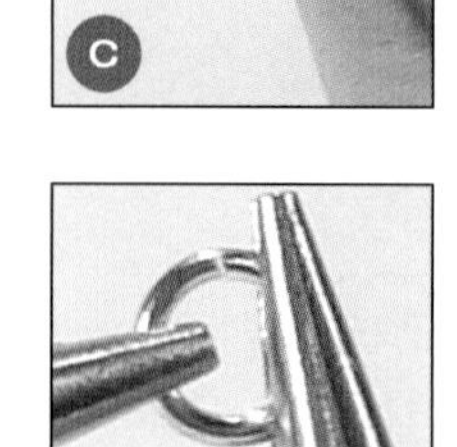

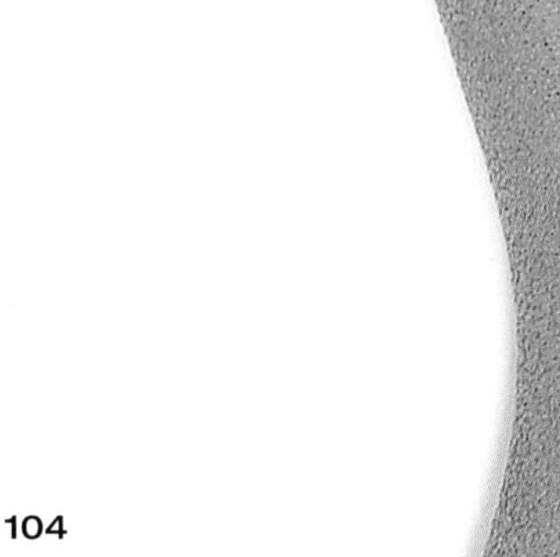

Crimp Cover

1 Use roundnose pliers to gently open the crimp cover.

2 Place the crimp cover over the folded crimp and gently squeeze shut with chainnose pliers.

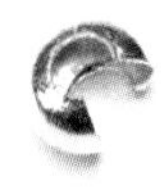

Attaching a Clasp

1 For a two-piece clasp, on each end, string: two crimp beads, Wire Guardian (optional), half of a clasp. Check the fit, and add or remove beads if necessary. Go back through the crimp beads and tighten the wire. Crimp the crimp beads and trim the excess wire **A**.

2 Or, follow step 1 to attach a lobster claw clasp on one end **B** and a soldered jump ring or chain extender on the other.

Tip—When using Wire Guardians, squeeze the ends together before crimping.

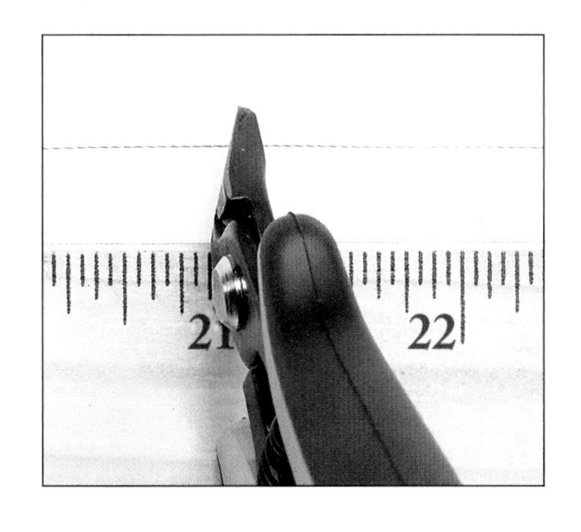

Cutting Flexible Beading Wire

Decide how long you want your necklace to be. Add 6 in. and cut a piece of beading wire to that length (for a bracelet, add 5 in.).

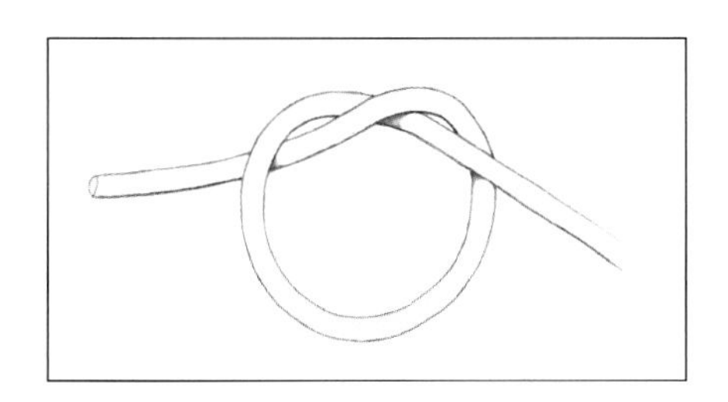

Overhand Knot

Make a loop and pass the working end through it. Pull the ends to tighten the knot.

Viking Knit

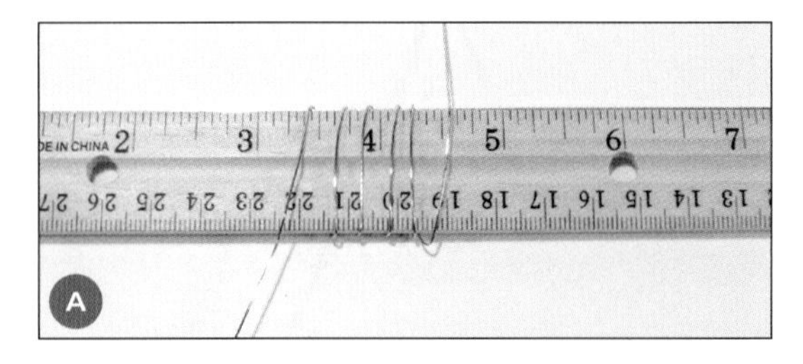

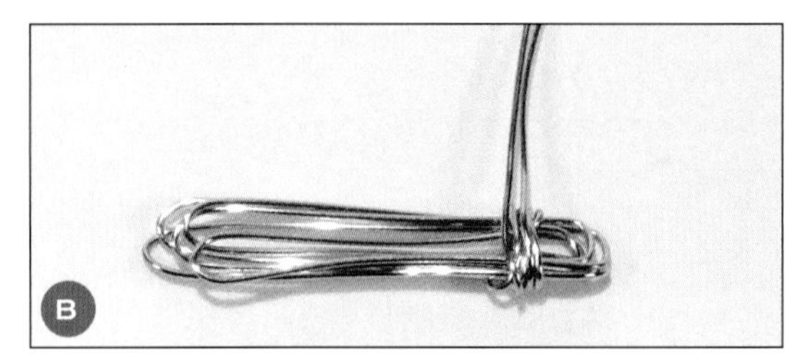

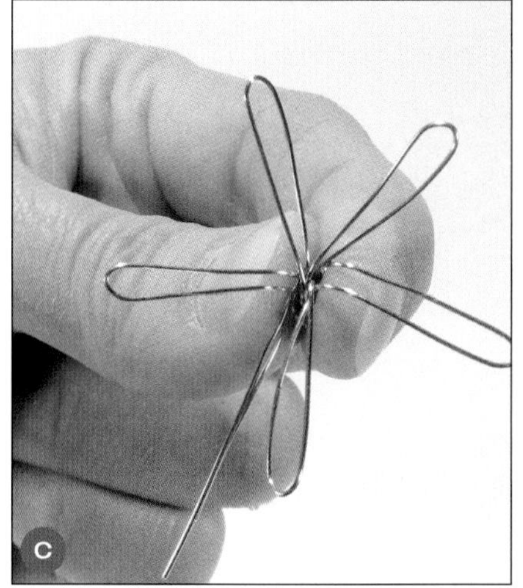

Getting Started

1 Wrap copper waste wire around a ruler four full times, leaving a 6-in. tail **A**.

2 Slide the loops off the ruler, squeeze the loops together, and wrap the tail wire around the bundle approximately 1/4 in. from the end **B**.

3 Open the loops to make a "daisy flower" **C**.

4 Place the daisy on top of an Allen wrench and evenly distribute the five petals. It is okay if the petals are slightly different in size. Optional: tape the petals to the allen wrench to secure **D**.

5 Cut 18 in. of 26-gauge wire. To begin, insert the wire down through one of the copper loops **E**.

6 Gently pull the wire down over the wire tail and up towards the next loop on the right using your left thumb to hold the wire tail in place to make the first loop of silver wire **F**.

7 Continue clockwise, making the first row of single-stitch Viking knit by placing the silver wire and inserting it down through the next loop then over the wire swag until you have reached the beginning **G**.

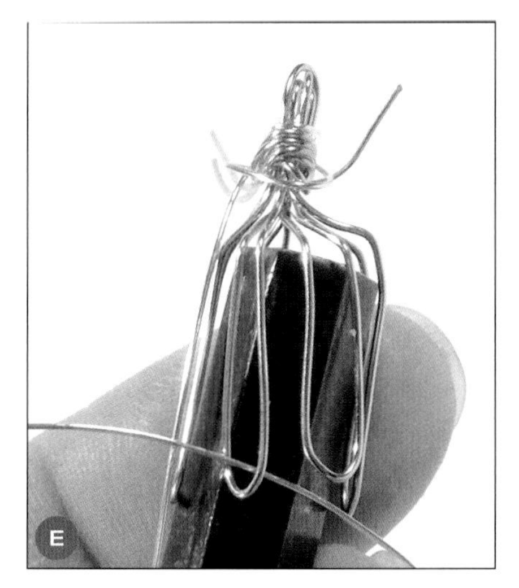

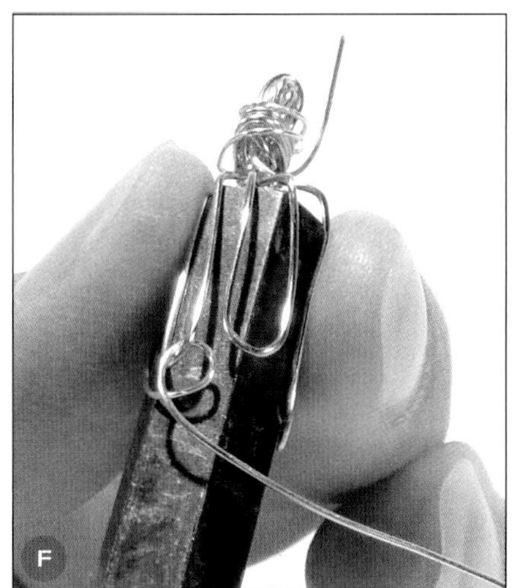

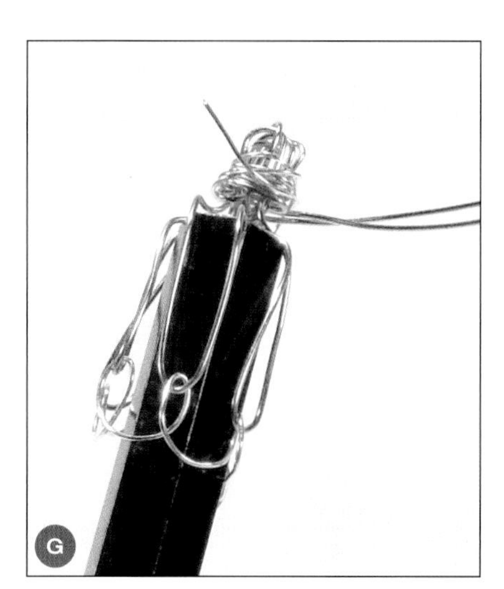

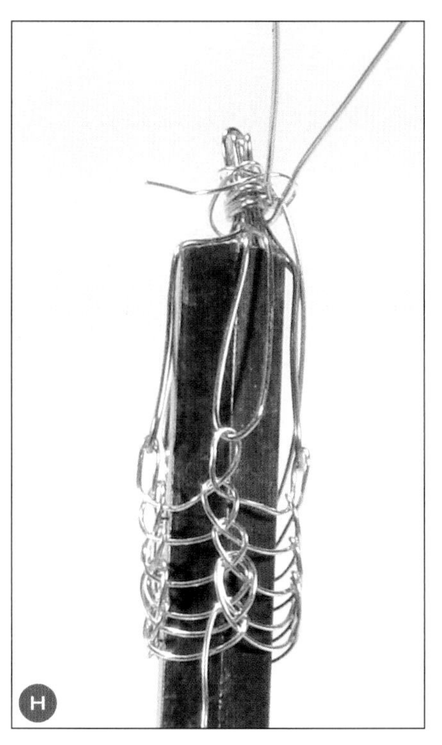

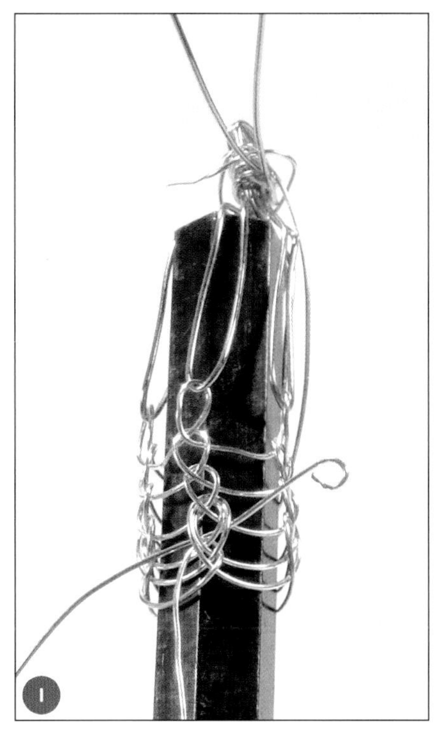

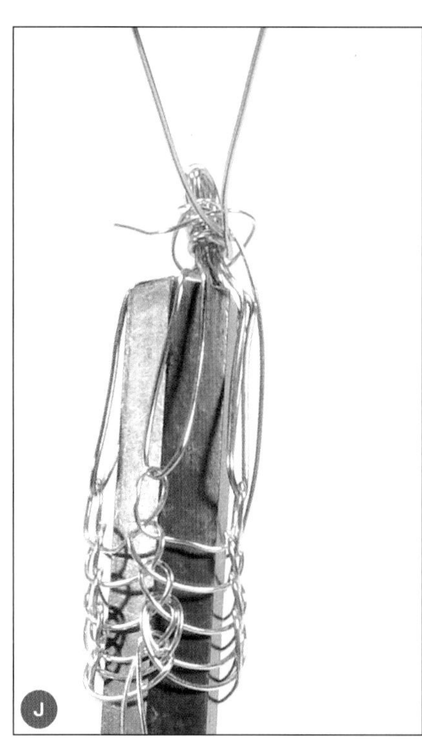

Adding Wire

8 To add new wire, lay the working wire that is too short or hardened straight down the Allen wrench **H**.

9 Cut a new 18-in. piece of 26-gauge sterling silver wire and make are very small hook on the end using the micro roundnose pliers **I**.

10 Insert the wire on the right side **J**.

11 Let the hook catch behind the X of where the wire ended and pull it out through the left side and continue with the Viking knit stitch. There is no need to cut the excess working wire as it will not affect the end product.

References

Middle Eastern and Venetian Glass Beads by Augusto Panini. Skira, 2007.

The History of Beads: From 30,000 B.C. to the Present by Lois Sherr Dubin. Thames and Hudson, 1995.

Collectible Beads: A Universal Aesthetic by Robert K. Liu. Ornament, 1995.

The Living Museum, vol. 65 no. 1, Spring 2003 by Jonathan E. Reyman.

Venice & The Veneto by Sylvie Durastanti and Angelo Lomeo with Sonja Bullaty. Abbeville Press, 1998.

Photo Credits

Nicole Anderson, Venice, Italy Trade seed beads cards (photo 1 page 13).

Collection of the Illinois State Museum, Photograph by Jason Arnold, ISM
ISM Accession #: 1954-0045 (photo 4 page 13).

All other travel and bead making pictures and all process photography, David Fox.

Project Sources

Beadalon
beadalon.com

Bella Venetian Beads
bellavenetianbeads.com

Chelsea's Beads
chelseasbeads.com

C-Koop
ckoopbeads.com

Dakota Stones
dakotastones.com

Robert Jennik
RobertJennik.com

Parawire
parawire.com

Pizazz Beads LLC (steampunk)
pizazzbeads.com

The Place to Bead
theplacetobead.com

Saki Silver
sakisilver.com

Sojourner
sojourner.biz

Fruit and vegetable market in Venice.

Gondolas on the Grand Canal.

Apartment in Venice above a store.

Quiet canal in Murano.

Measurement Conversion		
multiply	... by	... to find
inches	25.4	millimeters
millimeters	.04	inches
inches	2.54	centimeters
centimeters	.40	inches
feet	30.5	centimeters
centimeters	.03	feet
yards	.9	meters
meters	1.1	yards

This cuff bracelet, by Vonna Contino Maslanka, includes a white gold Miro oval bead and freeform beading on bison-back leather and denim.

About the Author

Kathy began her professional career with Eastman Kodak Company as a sales account executive. After working with Kodak for almost 10 years she retired from corporate life to stay home and raise her two children, Allison and Andrew. When her youngest was in school full time, she sought a career with more flexibility and in 2002, Kathy and her husband David opened The Place to Bead in Naperville, Ill., the first full service bead store in the area. During her search for unique and eye-catching beads for the store, Kathy developed a passion for Venetian beads, their history, and the Venetian culture. In 2004, Kathy and David expanded the business with the addition of Bella Venetian Beads and are now the largest importers of genuine Venetian beads in the country.

Kathy sightseeing in San Marco Square by Doge's Palace.

Florist in Venice.

David Fox, photographer, at Rialto Bridge.

Kathy wants to help maintain the integrity and history of Venetian beads and has been a guest speaker at NAJA National Association of Jewelry Appraisers (Tucson show, Feb. 2009) and the Gemological Institute of America Alumni Manhattan Chapter (spring 2009) to share this information. She continues to manage and teach classes at The Place to Bead and also is the show promoter for the biannual Suburban Bead Encounter. Kathy enjoys traveling to Europe and in 2008 organized a Mediterranean Bead Cruise with land excursions to Venice, Murano, Torcello, and Burano. Kathy resides in Naperville with her husband David, their children, and two dogs. In her spare time Kathy enjoys attending her daughter's soccer games in Florida, her son's baseball games and tournaments, volunteering at ADOPT (Animals Deserving Of Proper Treatment) and is planning another bead cruise.

Acknowledgments

Thank you to my family for their support while I wrote this book especially David, my husband, for the many hours he endured with me taking project pictures (book #32 is yours), his parents, Bob and Beryl, for being built-in babysitters allowing me to travel worry-free, and finally my mom and dad for making me the person I am today.